Thomas Macdonald

A Treatise on Civil Imprisonment in England

Thomas Macdonald

A Treatise on Civil Imprisonment in England

ISBN/EAN: 9783743686885

Printed in Europe, USA, Canada, Australia, Japan

Cover: Foto ©ninafisch / pixelio.de

More available books at **www.hansebooks.com**

A TREATISE

ON

CIVIL IMPRISONMENT IN ENGLAND;

WITH

THE HISTORY OF ITS PROGRESS,

AND

OBJECTIONS TO ITS POLICY,

AS IT RESPECTS

THE INTERESTS OF CREDITORS,

AND

THE PUNISHMENT, OR PROTECTION OF DEBTORS.

CONCLUDING WITH

THE PRINCIPLES AND GENERAL LINES OF A PLAN FOR AMENDING THE PRESENT LAW;

AND

AN APPENDIX OF NOTES.

By THOMAS MACDONALD, Esquire,
OF THE INNER TEMPLE, BARRISTER AT LAW.

LONDON:

PRINTED FOR J. MURRAY, N° 32, FLEET STREET.

M,DCC,XCI.

ADVERTISEMENT.

FROM some late discussions it would seem that the present laws of arrest upon actions, and of imprisonment for debt, are yet considered by many as, upon the whole, productive of general good consequences. The author of this treatise, which was written upwards of two years ago, has therefore been induced to publish it. He has endeavoured to place the subject in all the different points of view of which it was susceptible; and might have added a regular plan for amending that branch of the law, which his inquiries and reflections had enabled him to form.—But, in the present mode of communication, he has thought it more becoming to offer only the *principles* and general ideas on which that plan proceeds. These will be found in the concluding chapter. Its objects are, by means of a plain and practical course of proceeding, to render imprisonment for debt more beneficial to the fair creditor; and less oppressive to the honest debtor.—On the one hand, to remove as much as possible the creditor's just complaint of its inefficacy as a remedy; and on the other, to preclude every argument, on the part of the debtor, for the necessity of such occasional acts of insolvency as have of late been so wisely reprobated.

TO

THE RIGHT HONOURABLE

FRANCIS, LORD RAWDON,

BARON RAWDON, OF RAWDON,

IN THE COUNTY OF YORK,

&c. &c.

MY LORD,

WHEN I do myself the honour of inscribing the following little work to your Lordship, I cannot presume to think that by any expression of *my* perfonal refpect I fhall add to the general eftimation in which you are juftly held—But I gratify myfelf—And, if I had no fuch motives as act upon my mind with regard to your Lordfhip, the idea of placing your name at the head of a Treatife on Civil Imprifonment would naturally fuggeft itfelf. The exertion you made for obtaining an alteration of our municipal law on that important fubject ought not foon to be forgotten.

For my part, knowing, as I do, thofe fentiments of juft and correct humanity, and that liberal, yet guarded reafoning on which your Lordfhip proceeded,

DEDICATION.

ceeded, I cannot refrain from saying, that you there displayed a public spirit, of that character and description, which it is not flattery to extol.

I have the honour to be,

With great respect,

MY LORD,

Your Lordship's most obedient,

And most humble servant,

Inner Temple,
March 1791.

THO^S MACDONALD.

PREFACE.

THE author of the following treatise knows little of his own mind, if any thing it contains can justly be ascribed to a presumptuous and intemperate spirit of reformation; which, even in matters of municipal law, abjures all respect for established practice. He admires the genius of that philosophy which resists the prejudices of habitual opinion, and penetrates to the true character of things: but he is well convinced that its reasonings are often too abstract for application; and that the good to be derived in particular instances from frequent alterations of fixed and familiar laws, would upon the whole be far overbalanced by the uncertainty arising from perpetual fluctuation. Yet the timid pedantry of that submission which too often fetters the minds of men, has nothing in it to bear the test of candid reflection. Bending to every absurdity with implicit obedience, it denies to society all the benefits of experience; and aims preposterously at holding stationary, what must for ever be progressive.

PREFACE

Numberless are the instances which might be mentioned of long subsisting errors or defects in most important laws, both civil and criminal; such as could not, but for the lazy habits of prejudice, have been suffered to remain for any length of time. Till the year 1690[*] a landlord who had taken or distrained his tenant's goods for rent could not by any possible means sell or dispose of them for his payment. Till 1702 [†], in trials for treason or felony, the witnesses for the prisoner were examined without oath; while the testimony of those against him had all the credit of that solemnity. Till the year 1706 [‡], a person convicted of a crime which the law held to be clergyable; that is, such as ought not for the first offence to be punished with death, was nevertheless hanged, if it happened that he had not been taught to read. It was not till the same year 1706, that those gross and palpable practices which disgraced the course of judicial proceedings, and formed the subject of the amending statute of Queen Anne § (penned and introduced by the great Lord *Somers*) were lopped off, or in part reformed. And till so late a period as 1727 ‖ the simple case of two contending parties having mutual debts was unprovided for; so that instead of setting off the one demand against the other, and having one judgment for the balance, two distinct actions

---

[*] 2 William and Mary, st. 1. c. 5.   [†] 1 Anne, st. 2, c. 9.
[‡] 5 Anne, c. 6.   § 4 Anne, c. 16.
‖ 2 Geo. 2. c. 22.

and

PREFACE. xiii

and judgments were neceffary. Thefe are but examples.

The exifting laws of *civil imprifonment*, or, in other words, the laws which in this country give to plaintiffs and to creditors certain powers over the perfons of defendants, only becaufe plaintiffs make oath in fupport of their claims, and of infolvent debtors, *only becaufe they are infolvent*, without even profeffing any purpofe of difcrimination, form a fyftem, in all its parts, fo fingular, and apparently fo repugnant to the general fpirit of our jurifprudence, that the author of this treatife could not refrain from making an exertion to bring it fully before the public.——But he would not be mifunderftood.—He is aware of that dangerous fpecies of bigotry which wears the character of liberal opinion; and, while he reprobates the laws of arreft and civil imprifonment, as they now ftand, he accedes without hefitation to the following pofitions.

1ft. That no law or eftablifhed legal practice ought to be altered or fuppreffed, till by clear demonftration it is fhewn to be effentially pernicious; and that the hiftory of fuch a law or legal practice, however clearly its origin and extenfion may be thereby fhewn to have arifen from an abufe of form or perverfion of principle, ought only to have the effect of meeting that prejudice, or fuperftitious reverence,

reverence, which precludes enquiry.—beyond that point it ought not to weigh.

2dly, That no law whatever, however neceffary or wife it may be, can ftand the teft of reafoning from extreme cafes of private hardfhip or injuftice fuffered by individuals under its abufe.

3dly, That whatever may have been anciently the cafe, the arreft and fudden imprifonment of debtors, or thofe who are folemnly charged as fuch, are now, *in certain circumftances,* indifpenfably neceffary.

And laftly, that a *fair* creditor is rarely a vindictive oppreffor of his unfortunate debtor; and that fraudulent or difhoneft debtors, are far more numerous than cruel creditors.

It was with the full impreffion of thefe truths upon his mind that the author proceeded to confider the prefent fubject, and treated it in the manner he has done. Every prefumption is in favour of a fyftem, which, though frequently the fubject of complaint, has yet fubfifted for centuries. It was therefore neceffary, by defcribing its origin and accompanying it in its courfe, to fhake the afcendancy which, to the exclufion of fair reafoning, it had gained. The frequency of fraud, and the grofs violations of common honefty and juft fentiment, which the unprincipled and ungrateful conduct of many debtors was for ever prefenting to the general view,

view, served to keep back the miseries of innocent and unfortunate men, who suffered as insolvent debtors, from the attention which in justice they deserved. It was therefore necessary to bring them forward to observation in the circumstances which truly belonged to them. By a misapplication of the principle, That no law is to be censured because injustice may be practised under its abuse, every law, however noxious and unjust, if not always the instrument of iniquity, might be placed beyond the reach of objection. It was therefore necessary to shew that the root of the evil was the want of principle and consistency in the law; that the various mischiefs it produced arose, not from it abuse, but from its regular execution; that it swept over all, without discrimination; was less frequently beneficial to the honest creditor, than convenient for the extortioner; and in sometimes promoting the ends of justice, promoted them by chance.

It still remained to anticipate those arguments which, in order to balance what cannot be the subject of dispute, ingenious men are ready to support upon speculative ideas of some general good. With that view it was only necessary to try the law in question upon principles of general policy.

But having gone so far, it became proper to go farther; for to prove that an evil exists, without offering the means of remedy, is but an unprofitable

use

use of words. The concluding chapter, therefore, suggests certain principles and ideas, with a view to the formation of a new law, for the great ends of protecting the unfortunate; punishing the dishonest; inducing the discharge of debt; and checking the extravagance of credit.

CONTENTS.

CONTENTS.

PART I.

CHAP. I.

THE Establishment of the Superior Courts of Law — — Page 1

CHAP. II.

The Origin of the different Modes of bringing Parties before the Courts of King's Bench and Common Pleas — — — 6

CHAP. III.

The extreme Forbearance, with regard to Personal Liberty, of the antient Proceedings at Law, in Civil Matters — — — 9

CHAP. IV.

A Reflection — — 11

CHAP. V.

The first Law of Imprisonment for a Civil Injury, unaccompanied by Force, introduced in favour of the BARONS — — 12

CHAP. VI.

The next Law of Civil Imprisonment introduced in favour of the MERCHANTS — — 15

CHAP. VII.

Another Law of Imprisonment in favour of the BARONS. — — — 19

CHAP. VIII.

Civil Imprisonment further extended by the Legislature — — — 21

CHAP. IX.

The Law of Imprisonment still further extended in Practice; but not by the Legislature — 24

CHAP.

CONTENTS.

CHAP. X.

The same Subject continued — 28

CHAP. XI.

The Law of Imprisonment still extended by the Legislature — — 31

CHAP. XII.

The Benefit of Summons or Warning, previous to the Arrest and Imprisonment of Defendants, taken away by new Contrivances, founded upon Supposition and Fiction — — 33

CHAP. XIII.

The Maxim " IN FICTIONE JURIS CONSISTIT " EQUITAS." — — 36

CHAP. XIV.

Bail for the Appearance of Defendants—or " BAIL " TO THE SHERIFF." — 38

CHAP. XV.

The imperfect Remedy applied by the Legislature, to Abuses practised under the Law of Bail, in the Reign of Charles the Second — — 41

CONTENTS.

CHAP. XVI.

The Effects of the Statute of CHARLES THE SECOND, *upon the Warrants of Arrest and Imprisonment of the Court of King's Bench* — 43

CHAP. XVII.

The Law of Civil Imprisonment, so far as it respects the Arrest of Defendants, or, technically, Imprisonment on MESNE PROCESS, *brought down to the present Time* — — 46

CHAP. XVIII.

Civil Imprisonment IN EXECUTION; *or Imprisonment of* DEBTORS — — 48

PART II.

CHAP. I.

*T*HE *general Purpose of the following Chapters* — — — 50

CHAP.

The immediate Effect of the Laws of Civil Imprisonment upon the Situation of the Individual — with a Reflection on the Prejudice arising from false Ideas of HUMANITY — — 52

CHAP. III.

The Blind Operation of the Laws of Civil Imprisonment — — — 55

CHAP. IV.

A simple Affidavit of Debt, the single preliminary Proceeding upon which a Defendant is arrested and imprisoned, on the Commencement of the Action against him — — — 58

CHAP. V.

The Question stated, Upon what PRINCIPLE *the Relation between Debtor and Creditor,* WITHOUT ANY CIRCUMSTANCE OF FRAUD, *draws after it the Consequence of that Imprisonment to which, by the Law as it stands, Debtors are subjected* — 60

CHAP. VI.

Civil Imprisonment in Execution considered as a PUNISHMENT — — 62

CHAP. VII.

Civil Imprisonment in Execution considered as a Mode of COERCION — — — 67

CHAP. VIII.

Civil Imprisonment in Execution considered as in itself a Legal SATISFACTION *to the Creditor* · 69

CHAP. IX.

Civil Imprisonment considered upon the Principle of an implied or tacit Agreement — 73

CHAP. X.

Civil Imprisonment considered with a View to the established legal Presumption of fair Intention, 'till the contrary is proved —, — 78

CHAP. XI.

The Deference justly due to Reasons of POLICY, *or general Utility, upon this Subject* 81

CHAP. XII.

Reasons of POLICY *against the present Law of Civil Imprisonment founded upon the Authority of the* BANKRUPT *Laws* — — 82

CHAP.

CHAP. XIII.

Thoughts on the proper Influence of Municipal Law, over the selfish Propensities of private Individuals; and on the general Nature and Circumstances of CREDIT—*introductory to certain other Reasons of* POLICY *against the Laws of Civil Imprisonment*
90

CHAP. XIV.

The same Subject continued — — 93

CHAP. XV.

Reasons of POLICY *against these Laws, as rather tending to encourage than restrain an* EXCESSIVE FACILITY OF CREDIT, *and the Progress of Extravagance* — — 95

CHAP. XVI.

Reasons of Policy against these Laws, as affording Temptations to the Commission of Extortion and Fraud; by affording the ready Means of Oppression. 100

CHAP. XVII.

Reasons of Policy against the present Law of Imprisonment for Debt, founded upon its known Inefficacy, as a general Remedy, to the fair and honest Creditor.
103

CHAP.

CHAP. XVIII.

The Law of Imprisonment for Debt considered with a View to the present State of those Frauds which it was meant to restrain — 105

CHAP. XIX.

The remarkable Provision contained in the Statute commonly called the LORDS ACT — 108

CHAP. XX.

An Argument founded upon the frequent Institution of CHARITABLE SOCIETIES *for the Relief of insolvent Debtors in Prison* — 112

CHAP. XXI.

Acts of Insolvency — — 115

CHAP. XXII.

RECAPITULATION — — 119

CHAP. XXIII.

Conclusion. — *Containing* THE PRINCIPLES AND GENERAL LINES OF A PLAN *for amending the Laws of Civil Imprisonment* — 122

CONTENTS

OF THE

APPENDIX.

THE *Jurisdiction of the Court of Common Pleas; the Nature of different Writs; and the ancient Course of Proceedings in Actions*   Page 145 *et seq.*

Chapter 29 *of Magna Charta,* "Nullus liber homo," &c. — — — 148

Mr. Burgess's "*Considerations upon the Law of In-*"*solvency*" — — 149

Ancient Proceedings in the Case of Bailiffs *or* Accountants — — — 149

The

The Statute of Merchants — 150

Statutes *against Bailiffs or Accountants* 155

Lord Coke's Obfervation upon the Proceedings of Edward the Firft againft his Judges — 156

A material Difference in Effect between commencing certain Actions in the Court of King's Bench by Bill, *and commencing them by* Original Writ 157

Obfervation by Lord Mansfield, *and Quotations upon the Subject of legal* Fictions *and Subtleties* 159

The Abufes mentioned in the Statute of the 8th *of Elizabeth* — — 160

The Defcription of Abufes and Oppreffions by Arreft, in the Statute of the 13th *of Charles the Second* 161

The Statutes requiring an Affidavit of Debt to the Amount of Ten Pounds, previous to an Arreft 162

Inftances of abfurd and oppreffive Imprifonments ftated in the Preamble of 25 *Geo.* III. *c.* 45—*and the limited Imprifonments for fmall Debts under that Statute* — — 164

Note of the Law, which, by putting into the Creditor's Hands the Perfon, *withdraws from him the* Eftate *of the Debtor* — — — 165

The

APPENDIX. xxxii

The Law of Civil Imprisonment in Scotland, *brought down from its first Establishment to the present Time* — — — 166

The Law of Civil Imprisonment in Holland, *and in the trading Cities of* Germany — 177

The Marquis of Beccaria *on Imprisonment* 178

Puffendorff *and* Barbeyrac *on Insolvency* — 179

The Prisons filled, in the Reign of Charles the Second, with Persons who had been ruined by the Civil Wars, *and* the Fire of London — 180

The Statute of Richard the Second for preventing Debtors from enjoying too much of " the Sweet" *of Imprisonment* — — 181

A Prison a good Situation for a Miser—his Riches are secured to him by the Imprisonment of his Person, and he can there enjoy the Poverty of others — 182

Authorities to shew that the Imprisonment of the Debtor is considered, in law, *as being of itself* " *an ample* " *Satisfaction to the Creditor"* — 183

Barbeyrac, Bynkerfhock, *&c. upon the Power of Creditors over the Persons of their Debtors among the* Romans — — 184

Persons

CONTENTS, &c.

Persons infane, *arrested as Defendants, and kept in Prison as Debtors — the Law cannot release them* 185

Puffendorff *upon the Insolvency of* Merchants 186

An Observation on the Abuse of the Bankrupt Laws 187

An Extract from the Lords Act — 188

Remarkable Facts appearing from the Reports and Proceedings of the Society for the Relief and Discharge of unfortunate Persons imprisoned for Small Debts 192

The Practice as now established requiring Security for eventual Costs from Plaintiffs residing without the Reach of the Laws of England — 195

A TREATISE

A TREATISE

ON

CIVIL IMPRISONMENT IN ENGLAND.

PART I.

CHAP. I.

The Eſtabliſhment of the Superior Courts of Law.

THE ſuperior courts, which have been long eſtabliſhed in England for the various purpoſes of judicial adminiſtration, are at this day, as courts of original juriſdiction, the nobleſt ſeats of juſtice in the world. If they have not been always ſo—if there have been times when they were defiled by corruption, or diſgraced by ignorance, the people can look back, and, with a fuller ſatisfaction, rejoice in the ſure poſſeſſion of whatever rights the laws of their country have given them.

The old *Saxon* juriſdictions, which, under the ſyſtematic policy of *Alfred*, had diffuſed the equal adminiſtration

ministration of justice over the remotest parts of the kingdom, were superseded or abolished by the *Aula Regis* of the Conqueror. The judges of that great tribunal were the king, the chief justiciar, the great officers of state, and the greater barons of parliament. Substantially therefore, and in truth, the distinct functions of magistracy, and of legislation were engrossed and exercised by the same persons. In a collected body, with the king at their head, and under his direction, they made laws. They were then the great council of the nation, and obtained the name of Parliament. In separate committees they applied the laws: they were then considered as the judges of several courts.

The chief justiciar presided over their deliberations. He was the next man to his sovereign in rank, and often superior to him in consequence. Certain persons learned in the laws, called the king's justices, were appointed to instruct these great men in the law upon the subjects before them; but it did not follow that the law was to be so applied — the rights of the parties were often a secondary object.

In this state of things it frequently happened that the private contests among the people were either left to work themselves off in the violence of animosity and discord, or to be brought from the most distant parts, before this royal court, which followed the person of the king wherever he went. It was therefore one of the provisions of Magna Charta, that the Common Pleas, respecting the rights and transactions

ON CIVIL IMPRISONMENT.

transactions of the people among themselves, should not follow the king, but be determined in some certain place. Thus a branch was, in effect, split off from the *Aula Regis*, and a distinct court of *Common Pleas* became stationary in Westminster hall*.

Yet the *Aula Regis* was still a vast and unwieldy machine, the unequal pressure of which was severely felt. It had long affected the power of the sovereign, as well as of the people: for those who held the administration of justice (as that which went under the name of justice was then administered) held the command of the kingdom. But this could hardly be seen by men who, blinded by the rude passions, the gross superstitions, or the narrow ambition, of barbarous times, had therefore no clear ideas of their own interests. It was *Edward the first* who discovered the necessity of breaking down the *Aula Regis*, for the support of royal authority. But to divide its powers without losing them, was a task which called for all his vigour and ability.

In delegating the functions of magistracy, it naturally occurs, that certain subjects can hardly be brought under the immediate inspection of the sovereign himself. Such subjects comprehend the various questions which arise in the civil affairs of the people, and require a minute and laborious attention to all those intricacies in the application of municipal law, which sooner or later, in every state,

* See Hargrave's notes on 1 Inst. note 2. 71 b.

resolve

resolve themselves into a science; increasing in magnitude and difficulty, as the rights of the people increase in value and variety. The superintendance, management, and controul of public revenues and accounts, form another branch, which cannot come under the immediate care of a monarch. But when these different articles are delegated, those which remain are the fit and necessary objects of his peculiar attention. As the father, and protector of his people, it is his duty to guard from injury the lives and persons of his subjects: as the great keeper of the peace of the public, he is bound to watch over its preservation.

It is the chief character of every wise establishment, to follow and give effect to the natural order of things. The distinct departments under which the objects of judicial authority thus naturally ranged themselves, were therefore wisely reduced into a regular system of policy by Edward. While he founded, or rather restored, a variety of inferior jurisdictions, or subordinate ministerial offices, for the necessary purposes of spreading abroad over the different parts of the kingdom, and extending to causes of all civil descriptions, the salutary powers of justice, the greater and more weighty subjects of investigation were formed, in the above order, into three superior * jurisdictions. The first-mentioned branch of affairs fell under the jurisdiction of the

---

* The word *superior* is used, because the great barons of parliament still retained the *supreme* appellate jurisdiction over the kingdom.

Court

ON CIVIL IMPRISONMENT.

Court of *Common Pleas*, which had been before fixed at Westminster, by virtue of the Great Charter. The second was made the department of certain officers styled *Barons of Exchequer*, whose chief functions were more of a ministerial than a judicial nature, but who, in exercising their authority, respecting the king's accounts and revenues, over the king's accountants and debtors, soon acquired an ampler jurisdiction. Whatever remained of the functions of magistracy, still continued more immediately in the hands of the sovereign, and formed a royal jurisdiction, which comprehended not only such higher objects of cognizance as directly affected the lives and persons of individuals, or the peace of the public, but also the controul of inferior jurisdictions, and such causes of complaint as admitted of no precise definition, or had no other means of remedy. This high jurisdiction was exercised by a court in which the king himself was understood to preside. On that account, and in contradistinction to the Court of *Common Pleas*, or *Common Bench*, it was emphatically styled the Court of *King's Bench*; and possessed, inherently, such powers of legal discretion, superintendence, and pre-eminence, as were sufficient, in every possible case, to prevent a defect either of public or of private justice [*].

[*] The above is presented as no more than a general sketch of the origin of the superior courts; which the author has briefly drawn as proper introductory matter to his main subject. Particular descriptions of the courts will be found in *Bracton*, *Britton*, and *Fleta*; and most of the eminent writers of the law have treated of them fully and historically.

CHAP. II.

The Origin of the different Modes of bringing Parties before the Courts of King's Bench and Common Pleas.

THE establishment of different jurisdictions for the determination of private disputes, with the necessary powers for compelling obedience, gives effect to the due and regular course of law: but it also serves to introduce a species of trespass upon the peace of individuals, perhaps not much less dangerous in its consequences to the happiness of the people, than even the violence of open outrage. It is not then enough that the law provides means for the security of right, or the reparation of civil injury: it must likewise guard against their abuse; that they be not perverted for the purposes of levity, resentment, or extortion.

The judges of the Court of Common Pleas, acting purely by delegated authority, issued their process in general by virtue of a power expressly given them, in every particular instance, by special warrant, ordering the party to appear before them. They could not of themselves call parties before them*: that power still remained with the king, and was exercised by his officer who had the custody of his great seal, styled *the Chancellor*.

* Appendix, A.

Whoever

ON CIVIL IMPRISONMENT. 7

Whoever had a complaint againſt his neighbour in matter of civil right, was obliged to apply for the means of a remedy to the chancellor. His duty it was, in chancery, to hear the party complaining upon the particular nature of the complaint, and to give him a writ, or warrant, ſhortly deſcribing the cauſe (from which theſe writs were denominated *Brevia* *) directed to the ſheriff, for the purpoſe of obtaining ſatisfaction from the party, or his appearance before his majeſty's juſtices at Weſtminſter to anſwer to the charge. But the writ or warrant thus iſſued by the Chancellor was qualified with an expreſs condition that the plaintiff ſhould give ſecurity, by finding pledges or ſureties, for his proſecuting the ſuit with effect; ſo that if he proceeded without grounds, or from malice, he might be puniſhed by a fine to the king for this abuſe of the forms of juſtice, and treſpaſs upon the peace of his ſubject †. Till the plaintiff found good ſubſtantial ſecurity to that effect, for which the ſheriff was anſwerable, the ſuit could not be commenced.

Thus the Court of Common Pleas derived its power of proceeding from the ſpecial warrant or writ of the king, iſſued by his Chancellor ‡; and

---

* Appendix, B.   † Appendix, C.

‡ What is here ſtated applies to the general juriſdiction of the Court of Common Pleas in common actions, and when the parties were not officers, miniſters, or privileged perſons of the court. "Where ſuch perſons are parties, the Court of Common Pleas "may hold plea by bill, without any original writ;" and they may alſo grant prohibitions "to keep as well temporal as eccleſiaſtical courts within their bounds and juriſdiction, without any original or plea depending." 4 *Inſt.* 99.

that

that writ put a negative upon proceeding, if security was not given for a fair and *bonâ fide* prosecution of the suit.

No such preliminary warrant from Chancery was however necessary in the administration of the king's own reserved and pre-eminent jurisdiction respecting such matters of private right as were also of immediate public concern; and whatever contained in it any ingredient of criminality, was matter of immediate public concern, falling properly under that pre-eminent jurisdiction. There the sovereign exercised, by his judges, his own inherent functions; and precepts or warrants, of course, and in the first instance, issued from his own Court of *King's Bench*, for bringing delinquents, or persons accused of *forcible* injuries, before him *.

* See the mode of bringing defendants before the Court of *Exchequer*, Chap. X. *infra*.

CHAP. III.

The extreme Forbearance, with regard to Personal Liberty, of the antient Proceedings at Law, in Civil Matters.

THE original writ or warrant which issued from Chancery for bringing before the court the party charged with an injury purely civil, was directed to the sheriff; and it might naturally occur, that the law gave him power in all cases without distinction, in executing his warrant, to bring the party, if he disobeyed, before the court by force. But this was not the case—his warrant was only the original ground of certain writs and proceedings; the course and operation of which give a just idea of that excessive regard which in those days was paid to personal freedom, even in the exercise of the highest and most important powers of civil authority*.

After repeated acts of wilful disobedience and contumacy, by not appearing in court, the defendant was still suffered to be at large, and perfect master of his person; and as, perhaps, he never had any property to lose, or what he once had (which might have been sufficient to pay the debt) had gone to the king upon the writ of distress which issued for his disobedience, all the subsequent writs and war-

* The course of these writs and proceedings is stated in the Appendix, D.

rants

rants which fucceffively followed, were fulminated against a shadow.

If again the defendant obeyed the original writ, by appearing in court, and judgment paffed againft him, then ftill his eftate only was anfwerable—his perfon was free.

Such was the courfe of legal proceedings againft a man charged at the fuit of another with the breach of an obligation purely civil. But where the injury was attended with violence, and therefore the cafe had fomething criminal in its nature, or, as the law-books exprefs it, *favoured* of criminality, his perfon was not fo inviolably fecure, even where the proceedings, fubfequent to the original writ, iffued from the Court of Common Pleas. He was liable, in an action of that nature, eventually to imprifonment; but only in cafe he had no property to diftrain, and not till after repeated warnings had been given him *.

When a defendant, having been brought into court by force of diftreffes executed againft his effects, had judgment given againft him, he was ordered to pay a fine to the king for the public offence he had committed; and till that fine was paid †, he was detained in cuftody *on account of the public*; but ftill, if he fatisfied the king for the intereft of the public, the private creditor could only attach his property; he had no power whatever over his perfon.

* Appendix, E.   † Gilbert's Law of Executions, p. 59.

CHAP. IV.

A Reflection.

IT was a wild and unwarrantable liberty, which, in any cafe, fuffered a private individual to fet himfelf obftinately againft civil authority, by repeatedly contemning a lawful command, which it was at all times in his power to obey. The original complaint might not charge him with any circumftance of violence againft his neighbour; but he became criminal by his fubfequent conduct. His contempt made him an offender againft the public, and therefore fubjected his perfon to the coercive power of public authority. But if the original charge was for an injury attended with circumftances of force and outrage, his refufal to appear in court was a proof of his guilt; and the violence he had committed againft one, was fufficient to fhew that his liberty, while he remained unpunifhed, was dangerous to all.

Yet this extreme of perfonal freedom has been extolled as antient Englifh liberty—for as fuch it is defcribed in the declamations of thofe men, who, in viewing the rude and unprincipled fimplicity of former times, are for ever dreaming of the ideal felicity and vifionary virtues of a golden age.

The legal hiftorian can inform us, that the perfons of men were often placed beyond the reach of public reftraint, that they might be the furer victims of private flavery.

CHAP. V.

The first Law of Imprisonment for a Civil Injury, unaccompanied by Force, introduced in favour of the BARONS.

THE progress from that extreme of private personal freedom, which counteracted the necessary powers of civil authority, to its opposite extreme, which defeated their best purposes, is now to be traced.

It was only by degrees that the idea of depriving a man of his liberty in any case, where he had not forfeited it by the commission of some act of open violence, could insinuate itself into a system of laws which rose upon the foundation of a great charter of liberties*. In very early times, dishonesty, or a disregard of the rights of others, assuming one uniform rude and turbulent character, effected its purposes by forcible means; but when the rights of individuals were guarded by the powers of a social compact more closely united, and better braced, dishonesty had to steal towards its ends by secret artifice, falsehood, and treachery.

By degrees, therefore, the idea which had been before annexed to acts of open violence, extended itself to the impositions practised under all the different modes of fraud and artifice. But till the laws adopted that idea, it may well be conceived

* Appendix, F.

ceived what enormities were committed by men, who having no property to lose, and nothing to fear for their persons, committed them with impunity: yet it was some considerable time before the laws did adopt that idea. The complaints of the poor and dependent could seldom reach the seat of government; and in those days every man was poor and dependent who was not great.

It was not therefore till the great felt the evil that a remedy was thought of. It had become a common practice with bailiffs and receivers who collected the rents of the Barons, to abscond, without rendering an account of the sums they had received. In such a case the thought was natural, that the *person* of the man should be seized, for the purpose of compelling him to do what was clearly in his power, namely, *to render an account* of what he had received.

In the reign of *Henry the third* a law was accordingly passed*, by which it was enacted, That bailiffs who failed to account to their lords, *if* they withdrew themselves, *and* had no lands or tenements by the seizure of which they might be distrained upon the common writ of attachment, should "be attached by their bodies."

Natural and rational as the general idea of this law certainly was, the novelty of it seems to have induced a degree of caution, in applying the remedy, which rendered it nugatory, or, at least, extremely inadequate. The arrest of the defaulter's person could only, after all, take place where two circum-

---
* 52 Hen. III. c. 23. Stat. of Marlbridge.

stances

stances concurred. It was neceffary not only that he fhould have abfconded, but alfo that he fhould not have belonging to him a freehold eftate in lands or tenements, even to the moft trifling value *: for it was ftrictly interpreted as being a law againft liberty. If he either remained at home, or, rather choofing to go elfewhere with his booty, purchafed an acre of land within the county, to evade the ftatute, he might refufe to render an account, and his perfon was free as ever †.

* 2 Inft. 144.   † Appendix, G.

CHAP. VI.

The next Law of Civil Imprisonment, introduced in favour of the MERCHANTS.

IT was in the celebrated reign of Edward the first that the law first seized upon the personal liberty of a *mere debtor*. The same views of ambition which had led that able monarch to break down the grandeur of the *Aula Regis*, by annihilating its leader (the great justiciar of the kingdom) and separating its parts, taught him the expediency of advancing some new acting power in the state, which might put the balance into his own hands, and enable him to preserve or destroy the equilibrium at pleasure. The Barons, having long been the lords of the common people, were hardly the subjects of the king; and he saw that as long as the common people were the mere instruments of others, they would be the instruments of those who held over them the immediate means of oppression. It was therefore by extending the views, and raising the principles of the people at large, that he wisely thought of being indeed the monarch of his kingdom.

This could only be effected by enabling them to acquire rights and interests, under his patronage and protection, which should render them independent of their former oppressors: and these were only to be acquired by means of the extension and encouragement of *trade*.

But

But as the law then stood it was hardly possible to carry on the fair course of trade with safety. The chief consumers of every commodity were in those times the proprietors of land: they contracted large debts to the merchants: their lands were protected from execution by feodal principles; and the circuitous progress of *distresses*, even *distresses infinite*, as they were called, had the effect to encrease but not to remedy the mischief. Many of these distresses brought nothing to the creditor, but, on the contrary, carried off the very property which ought to have paid him. They were disregarded by some, who had no property to lose, and defeated by others, who held the corrupt ministers of the law in their interest. They formed, in short, too tardy and uncertain a course of procedure for the enforcement of that punctuality, which even the simplest ideas of trade soon shew to be indispensable towards the support of mercantile credit.

In the eleventh year, therefore, of that monarch's reign, the statute of *Acton Burnel*, as it is called, was passed; by which it was made lawful to a merchant, whose debtor had acknowledged his debt before a certain magistrate, to apply, after the day of payment, for a warrant to sell his debtor's moveables and chattels; or, if no buyer was to be found, to have them delivered up to him, at a reasonable price, towards satisfaction of the debt; and if the debtor " had no moveables whereupon the debt might be levied," the statute declared, that " his body should then be taken where it might be found, and kept in
prison,

ON CIVIL IMPRISONMENT. 17

prison, until that he had made agreement, or his friends for him."

Two years after, the remedy was farther extended, with much severity, by a new law*, explanatory of the former; by which the debtor of a merchant was, after the day of payment, made liable to immediate imprisonment, without regard to his effects; but with express power to him, at any time within a quarter of a year, to sell his lands or chattels for the purpose of discharging the debt; and after expiration of that quarter, all his lands and goods were to be delivered to the creditor, " by a reasonable extent;" the debtor's body being still kept in prison till payment of the debt by means of his estate; the creditor finding him bread and water for his sustenance. It was declared that the benefit of this statute should not extend to the JEWS.

Both these statutes have been understood as forming one entire law; both being entitled the *Statute of Merchants*, as exclusively in favour of that class of men; and its extraordinary severity against their debtors, arose from the circumstances of the times.

---

* 13 *Edward* I. *st.* 3. The preamble of this statute points out the *peculiar* object of the law in these words: " Forasmuch as *merchants*, which heretofore have lent their goods to diverse persons, be fallen in poverty, because there is no speedy remedy provided whereby they may shortly recover their debt at the day of payment; and for this cause many merchants do refrain to come into the realm with their merchandize, to the damage of such merchants and of all the realm."—As several parts of the statute may afford matter of observation, the whole of it will be found in the Appendix H.

C   The

The rising interests of trade required in those days the helping hand of government: for the merchant, who was not then, as he is now, the first private character in the state, had to struggle in the crowd against the contempt and injustice of the great. It was Edward's policy to bring him forward, by extraordinary legal privilege; and his policy was founded on public wisdom.

CHAP.

CHAP. VII.

Another Law of Imprisonment in favour of the Barons.

IT was not Edward's policy to attempt any sudden depression of the great men who surrounded his throne. He knew that they would fall, exactly as the commons rose; and it was only necessary to divert their attention from the turn which he had given to the balance.

The mercantile body had received signal marks of favour; and if the barons had not at the same time been soothed, they would, it is probable, have exerted all their power for the discouragement of that body of men; not as rivals of any note or consideration, but as being, in their estimation, unworthy and contemptible favourites.

The law which had been made in the last reign, for the purpose of compelling by imprisonment the bailiffs and receivers of the barons to render their accounts, was in itself a fit subject of amendment: for, even after the defaulter had complied with the law, by delivering an account, the substantial evil still remained. That account might shew a heavy arrear against him; and there the statute was silent. The Barons, therefore, now acquired a very strong remedy, giving them powers over the persons of their debtors, (for it may be presumed that, except their tenants, their receivers of rents were *their* only immediate

ate debtors) still more ample than those obtained by the merchants. It was enacted*, that their bailiffs and receivers, upon being found in arrear by the decision of auditors (who were appointed by these lords themselves) should be immediately committed to the nearest prison, where the sheriff, or his gaoler, was to keep them *in irons*; and where they were to live at their own expence, till they fully satisfied their lords for the arrears which they owed †.

These statutes against bailiffs, in matters of *account*, are material to the present purpose, as they are referred to in subsequent laws, extending imprisonment to other causes; but of themselves, they operated only within a very narrow circle, and were directed against one particular object. They went, indeed, beyond the line which had long been held sacred, and which protected every man from the loss of liberty, for any cause short of open outrage, or forcible injury: but they were also levelled against an act of the worst species of dishonesty; namely, a breach of trust, aggravated, in general, by a disregard of one of the strongest relations then known in the state.

* 13 Edward I. c. 11. † Appendix I.

CHAP.

CHAP. VIII.

Civil Imprisonment further extended by the Legislature.

FOR upwards of sixty years the law of imprisonment, for a cause purely civil, rested where it had been left by Edward the first, viz. with Barons who had been defrauded by dishonest stewards, and merchants, who required all the encouragement and aid which extraordinary privileges and protection could give. It operated upon such particular circumstances as at first justified its introduction, and afterwards facilitated its progress. The idea was no longer novel. The practice, in those special cases, had reconciled it, by habit, to the minds of the people. When, therefore, it was afterwards extended to others, it proceeded without observation; till at length it grew insensibly into a common course of execution.

In those days, the circle of contingencies, in the affairs of men, was more bounded than it is now; their connections were fewer; their transactions less complicated. The effects, therefore, of future events, were more within the range and foresight of prudence; and it followed, as a necessary consequence, that fewer honest individuals could be ruined by unforeseen calamities. In general, an insolvent debtor was then an unworthy member of society. So uncertain were the obligations which, in antient times, arose from implied engagements, that a *debt*, technically

nically so called, being a right to demand a *sum certain*, was founded on some public, or judicial, act, or written instrument; or such a contract, without writing, as might reduce the sum demanded to a certain precise amount. To debts of this determinate nature the *action of debt* was confined; and if it proceeded upon a written instrument, such as a bond or deed, the defendant could run little hazard of suffering by an erroneous or unjust judgment; because, if the debt had been paid, the bond or deed would have been cancelled. If it proceeded upon a simple contract, there was a privilege incident to the action, which indeed lay open to manifest objections in point of expediency as well as justice, but protected an honest defendant of fair character. He was permitted to clear himself of the demand, by swearing that he owed nothing; which was conclusive, if he got eleven of his neighbours (who were called *compurgators*) to support his credit, by making oath that they believed he swore truly. This was termed *waging his law**.

To this action of *debt* (for reasons perhaps founded upon the particular nature of such actions) and also to the action of *detinue*, in which the defendant had the same privilege of *wager of law*, the same process against the person of the defendant, which had been given to the Barons against their bailiffs; or, in other words, the law of imprisonment by arrest, was extended in the reign of Edward the third†.

* The source of this practice has been often traced, and is well known—Even now it is known *in law*.
† 25. Edward III. c. 17.

In

ON CIVIL IMPRISONMENT.

In the action of *detinue*, the nature of the injury had something criminal, or at least grofsly difhoneft, in its compofition. That action* lay againft a perfon who having, by fair means, or with the appearance of right, got the goods of another into his poffeffion, afterwards wrongfully detained them. He had not indeed poffeffed himfelf of them by theft or robbery; but, from the moment he refufed to reftore them to the right owner, he held them by no better title.

* Now fuperfeded in practice by the action of *trover*, in which there lies no wager of law: as the action of *debt*, on fimple contract, is, (partly, for the fame reafon), fuperfeded, in practice, by the action of *indebitatus affumpfit*, for breach of promife, or of *affumpfit*; which is the technical word for engagement or *undertaking*.

CHAP. IX.

The Law of Imprisonment still further extended in Practice; but not by the Legislature.

FOR some time after the establishment of the several courts of law, claims of right were most frequently both made and resisted with circumstances of force and violence, and the *proper* subjects of jurisdiction belonging to the Court of *King's Bench*, comprized, in those days, a great share of all the disputes which occurred among the people. An injury, in matter of private right, was then often truly, as well as technically, denominated a trespass *vi et armis*.

But the subjects of litigation changed of course with the manners of the people. Civil injury, without any mixture of violence, gave occasion to many actions; and as these were properly subject to the jurisdiction of the Court of *Common Pleas*, which had also cognizance of certain forcible injuries, by special warrant, or original writ *from Chancery* for each particular cause, that court soon came to determine most of the questions of private right which occurred.

The business of the Court of King's Bench was in this manner much abridged; and it would seem, that there have been judges who found less enjoyment in the honourable possession of their own proper pre-eminent jurisdiction, than in the constant exercise of judicial power, however trivial the subject.

The

The active spirit of industry began to be busy even on the bench; and its substantial gains soon bore down the dignity of magistracy*.

The chancellor, in exercising his power of issuing the king's original writs at the suit of the parties complaining, by which the Court of Common Pleas was authorized to take cognizance of causes, was frequently obliged to form new writs, according to the exigencies of particular cases, to which former precedents did not apply. This was indeed the subject of a special statute †; and an action founded upon any such newly-formed writ, was technically called an action of *trespass on the case*, to distinguish it from the action of trespass *vi et armis*, according to the different nature of the injury. For though both had the appellation of *trespass*, yet the trespass *vi et armis*, applied properly to an act which was " in itself an *immediate* injury to another's person or property." And the action *on the case* applied to an omission; or to an act which was not immediately, but only by consequence, and collaterally, injurious.

The various questions thus arising from the multiplicity of new rights, which the transactions of an improved society had introduced, were brought before either of the courts indifferently; according to the suggestion of the plaintiff at suing out his original writ from Chancery. And the Court of King's Bench came also frequently to act by a *delegated*, not an original authority, even in

---

* Appendix K. † 13 Edward I. c. 24.

judging of injuries which were held in law to be trespasses both against the private party and the public peace; and were consequently the proper subject of their own original jurisdiction*.

From that time, those lines of distinction which had been clearly and strongly marked out at the establishment of the courts, were rendered obscure and confused. The courts came soon to be rival powers, and were busily superseding the legislature by *fictitious* contrivances, which operated as new laws. Indeed, all their proceedings were sufficiently expressive of what was, in those days, their ultimate object—which was neither the protection of personal liberty; the security of property; the suppression of groundless litigation; nor the peace of the public.

The legislature, it has been observed, had already removed the natural impression (inconsistent, indeed, in its full extent, with the well-being of advanced society) that no civil power could touch the personal freedom of a man, who had committed no violent wrong, or offence against the peace of the public; and the people therefore were prepared to suffer the gradual progress of imprisonment, even for the declared purpose of preventing only a remote inconvenience.

The writs of trespass from Chancery came soon to be formed, with a view more to the process which might be convenient for the plaintiff, than to the nature of his complaint. Causes which had nothing in them of *trespass*, or active injury, but arose perhaps

* Appendix L.

from

from omiſſion, had yet been denominated treſpaſſes: and partly, perhaps, to favour the juriſdiction of the Court of King's Bench, or to divide the buſineſs of civil actions more equally; but chiefly, to authorize the impriſonment of the defendant, for which purpoſe a charge of violence was indiſpenſable, they were often feigned (without the ſmalleſt colour of truth) to have been attended with *force*.

Thus in numberleſs inſtances, before the legiſlature had extended impriſonment, a defendant was deprived of his liberty by the falſe application of a word.

CHAP.

CHAP. X.

The same Subject continued.

BY means of fictions, considerably bolder than that which has been just described, the laws of arrest and imprisonment were carried, in practice, still farther.

When a defendant was in the custody of the Court of King's Bench; that is, in prison, by its authority upon a charge of forcible injury, he might, if sued in another court, have got clear of that second action, by pleading the privilege arising from his being already in the custody of the Court of King's Bench*. Upon this a principle arose, that the court having him in custody for one sort of injury, was entitled to proceed against him for causes, of a nature totally different.

This principle, by a fiction contrived for the purpose, the officers of the court turned to good account. It was only *supposing* a man to be guilty of a trespass, or public offence, such as fell under the proper cognizance of the court, while perhaps they knew him to be innocent. The proper warrant of the court, viz. the *Bill of Middlesex*, (as it is generally termed) was issued for seizing his person immediately, and taking him into the custody of the court, that he might answer (as it was feigned) for

* Appendix M.

the

ON CIVIL IMPRISONMENT.

the *trespass* with which he was charged. He was brought accordingly, as a delinquent, before the court, and then given to understand, that the warrant had charged him with a supposed trespass, or forcible injury, for the sole purpose of entitling them to seize his person; and that now, being a prisoner, he was only to answer a complaint made against him by his neighbour, respecting a debt, or private transaction between them.

The Court of *Common Pleas* acted, of course, upon a similar plan, and proceeded upon a fictitious *trespass*, which authorized the subsequent process of imprisonment—for it is to be remembered, that without a charge of trespass, imprisonment, or *capias*, was no part of their process[*].

The Court of *Exchequer* proceeded also in a similar manner. Their jurisdiction was, in its original nature, strictly limited and very clearly defined. As mentioned in a former chapter, they had, ministerially, the management of the king's revenues, and judicially, the power of proceeding in matters respecting his debtors. When, therefore, they meant to exceed their jurisdiction, they *supposed* the plaintiff to be the king's debtor. Upon that false suggestion or fiction, they issued their own writ against the defendant, as being debtor to the king's debtor; averring, that the plaintiff, as the king's debtor, was *thereby the less*[†] able to pay the king's debt. Upon that

---
[*] See chap. 3, *supra*.
[†] The writ therefore obtained the name of *Quo minus*, from the introductory words of the sentence.

fiction,

fiction, *this debtor of the supposed debtor of the king*, was seized, imprisoned, and brought into court; and then the fiction had done its office*.

* The encouragement and indulgence which the spirit, either of litigiousness or rapacity, derived from this eagerness of practitioners, belonging to particular courts, to acquire employment, may be easily conceived—yet the fictions made use of to draw jurisdiction to different courts, in cases of which they had no legal cognizance, while they gave rise to many illegal imprisonments, may have been productive of one very important good consequence, as " they have probably," to use the words of Mr. *Mitford* in his treatise on the pleadings in Chancery, " had the effect of preventing that abuse of power which is too " often the consequence of the single jurisdiction of one supreme " court." The legislature however might, without the aid of fiction, have done the same thing.

CHAP.

CHAP. XI.

The Law of Imprisonment still extended by the LEGISLATURE.

FOR upwards of one hundred and fifty years, viz. from the 25th of Edward the third, to the 19th of Henry the seventh, the law of civil imprisonment was not extended by the legislature*—it was, on the contrary, alleviated in the reign of Henry the sixth, by the statutory introduction of bail to the sheriff, to be afterwards explained.

During that period, however, the industry of the practitioners of the law had been busily and profitably employed in fictitious practices, which were sometimes attended with certain salutary effects; but, in extending imprisonment, without law, were clearly unjustifiable. Those practices met at length indirectly with the approbation of the legislature. The law of imprisonment, by arrest of the defendant, was extended by statute † to all actions *upon the case* (as they were technically denominated) that is, to all such actions, proceeding, as already explained, upon original writs, for damages, arising consequentially from the particular circumstances of each particular case.

This was extending the law of imprisonment,

* Appendix N. † 19 Henry VII. c. 9.

without

without restriction or qualification, to almost every case which could occur*, and putting it far beyond the foresight of any man to guard against it.— Obligations in law arising from the most remote consequences, might at any time deprive him of his liberty.

But in former times, the particular genius of the monarch gave birth to particular laws for the government of the people; even where his own immediate interests did not require their aid. *It was in the reign of Henry the seventh* that the law thus extended the imprisonment of defendants upon mere civil demands. The spirit of avarice was then seated on the throne of England; and the rights of personal freedom; the independence of integrity; the efforts of industry; even the sacred claims of misfortune, were relentlessly sacrificed at her shrine. The reign of Henry the seventh became the petty tyranny of an extortioner; not the sovereignty of a monarch: and the people were taught, by the base ministry of *Empson* and *Dudley*, and the frigid maxims of their master, that a failure in the punctual payment of money, was a wrong, which no distinctions or circumstances could extenuate.

* It was afterwards, by 23 Henry VIII. c. 14. extended to actions of annuity and covenant.

CHAP.

CHAP. XII.

The benefit of Summons or Warning, previous to the Arrest and Imprisonment of Defendants, taken away by new contrivances, founded upon Supposition and Fiction.

IN such actions as proceeded upon an original writ from Chancery, the courts could only seize the person of the defendant by a subsequent writ of *capias ad respondendum* issued against him, eventually, and after the warning which preceding writs afforded him. The officers of the courts were thus frequently disappointed; as defendants who received such previous notice, had an opportunity of compromising claims, or appealing to the reason and humanity of creditors.

But they had also an opportunity of flying suddenly from their country like felons; of relinquishing their early habits; breaking the dearest ties of nature; and wandering forlorn in a land of strangers —for to this state of misery, it was said, a debtor would submit, rather than yield himself, a helpless prisoner, to answer for a debt he could not pay.

The practice of the courts, therefore, took a new course. By a chain of fictitious contrivances, they assumed the power of originating actions in such cases as, the law said, should only be originated by the king's writ from Chancery—plaintiffs were in substance, though not perhaps in form, delivered from the preliminary of finding *pledges of prosecution,* or security to the public, against groundless or malicious suits; and defendants were instantly seized by the officers of court, without notice, intimation, or warning of any sort; so that their "*bodies*" could not, by any possibility, be withdrawn from the united power of the plaintiff, the judge, and the gaoler.

The minds of the few who observed such innovations were diverted to considerations of the conveniency, which, it was said, would result from a practice correctory of the law—And the plan was carried into effect; thus—

An original writ from Chancery was supposed—Pledges of prosecution, or security against groundless and malicious suits, were supposed—the notice to the defendant was supposed—the sheriff's inquiry for goods was supposed—his answer or return, that the defendant had no goods, was supposed—And upon these various suppositions, of important facts[*], the writ for seizing the defendant's person issued on the instant; and, instead of being the very last, was the *first* proceeding against him. All the preceding steps were regularly taken *in law,* that is, (according to the meaning of the expression in many cases) they were not taken *in truth.*

The blow thus secretly and suddenly given, in every case, without regard to circumstances, it was impossible to ward off, even by fair and amicable means; and the credit and character of the defendant perhaps were ruined. But the officers of the court were made sure of emoluments,

* Append.x O.

ON CIVIL IMPRISONMENT.

which might otherwife have efcaped them. The legiflature knew nothing of thefe new laws; but the people were told " *In fictione juris confiftit equitas.*"—All obftructions or precautions in the way of fuitors, (becaufe fome had tended to the delay of juftice,) were now thrown down; and the body of a defendant, which might, it was faid, have been withdrawn from the plaintiff by voluntary banifhment, was thus fecured to him by imprifonment*.

* It need hardly be obferved, that whatever reflections may arife upon the conduct of the courts formerly, in not annihilating fees, but difpenfing with proceedings, which ftood, reafonably, between a mere defendant and imprifonment, and which it was their duty to have preferved wherever they had not been fuperfeded by ftatute; and however far it may be correctly juft to fay, that fuch practices were dangerous and illegal, it does by no means follow that thofe exploded proceedings ought now to be reftored in practice, or any thing fimilar to them adopted. It will appear from the fequel that they have not been ftated with any fuch purpofe in view.

CHAP. XIII.

The Maxim " IN FICTIONE JURIS CONSISTIT EQUITAS."

SUCH general maxims as communicate no precife idea, are weapons equally dangerous in the hands of perfidy and corruption, or of ignorance.

Thofe ftrange mifhapen powers, which prevailed in the reign of Charles the firft, practifed the worſt of their prepofterous follies and abufes, under the motto *" Salus populi fuprema lex."* The people were pleafed with the found; and never confidered that, of itfelf, it meant nothing, becaufe it defined nothing.

The wildeft latitude of opinion, or perverfion of udicial authority, has, at times, found fhelter under the adage *" Eſt boni judicis ampliare juſtitiam."*

The maxim *" In fictione juris confiſtit equitas,"* when taken as a general maxim, degrades the dignity of juftice, and is an infult to legiflative wifdom. Yet this maxim has, in the writings even of thefe days, been repeated and extolled as a propofition which every inftance demonftrates.

When from premifes which have no foundation in fact, but are fuppofed in law, a found conclufion is drawn, and a falutary effect produced, juſtice is adminiftered by the machinery of legal fiction. But
juftice

ON CIVIL IMPRISONMENT.

Juſtice diſdains to ſurrender her own natural character, or to diſtort her proceedings, by travelling through circuitous paths, to that which may be directly attained. Where the alternative is, that without the uſe of a fiction, in form, either the legiſlature muſt ſtrike at the root of a whole ſyſtem to get at a particular evil; or judges be compelled to ſtretch out the arm of authority in ſupport of palpable iniquity, the aſſiſtance of legal fiction is there to be permitted. But when legal fiction operates againſt the ends of juſtice, and the beſt principles of nature, it acts in oppoſition to the only purpoſe it can profeſs; and then deſerves another name *.

* See an obſervation on the ſubject of legal fiction, by *Lord Mansfield*, Appendix P.

CHAP. XIV.

BAIL *for the Appearance of Defendants—or* "BAIL TO THE SHERIFF."

THE personal liberty of defendants having become a lucrative subject of possession in the hands of the ministerial officers of the law, sheriffs and their followers *let to farm* the emoluments of their power—The consequences were dreadful. The country was over-run by bands of robbers, clad in the garb of office, and armed with the warrants of civil authority. The people were frightened at the name of their sovereign.

This had been the state of things for a long course of years, when, by a statute of Henry the sixth, some interruption was given to those depredations. By that statute * such offices were no longer to be let in farm; and persons arrested by the sheriff upon actions, were, agreeably to the common law, to be set at liberty, upon reasonable sureties, or *bail* for their appearance.

* 23 Hen. VI. c. 9.—The preamble of this statute shews the prevalence of those abuses which have been described above. It is in these words:. " Item, the king considering the great *perjury, extortion, and oppression,* which be and have been in this realm by his sheriffs, under-sheriffs, and their clerks, coroners, stewards of franchises, bailiffs, and keepers of prisons, and other officers, in divers counties of this realm, hath ordained by authority foresaid, in eschewing all such extortions, perjury, and oppression, that no sheriff," &c.

Yet

ON CIVIL IMPRISONMENT. 39

Yet they were only delivered from the hardships of immediate imprisonment. In fact, their persons were given up to their bail instead of the gaoler. If the defendant did not appear, the bail were answerable to the extent of the bail bond *.

If the statute, in giving the benefit of bail to defendants, had also restored that part of the common law which required security from plaintiffs for the fair and *bond fide* prosecution of actions; or had provided something equivalent, the remedy might have operated. But so long as it was in the power of a plaintiff to raise an action for any sum, without qualification or restraint, however groundless the demand, he could gratify his malice, or accomplish his purpose of extortion, by prosecuting for a sum far beyond the credit of the defendant—And the subsequent practice of the courts extended the evil; for, by virtue of their own discretionary powers, they required from the defendant substantial security, or, as it was termed, *special bail*, in all cases without distinction where the plaintiff stated his cause of action to amount to £. 20 or upwards; and afterwards, instead of raising the sum with the rise of money and the circumstances of the people, they reduced it to one half that sum; so that *common bail*, as it was termed, that is, the insertion of the fictitious names of Doe and Roe as

---

* This bail for the defendant's appearance can only be discharged by his giving bail, after the return of the writ, for the costs and condemnation; or that he shall render himself a prisoner.

securities, was admitted only where the debt appeared from the plaintiff's own state of it to be under £. 10. In that case the defendant, though liable to arrest, was discharged out of custody upon nominal bail; but wherever the debt was £. 10 or upwards, and he could not give substantial bail, or pay the money, he had no means of regaining his liberty.

CHAP.

CHAP. XV.

The imperfect Remedy applied by the Legiflature, to abufes practifed under the Law of Bail, in the Reign of Charles the Second.

THUS ftood the law and practice after the ftatute of Henry the fixth. The fuperior courts imprifoned the defendant for want of bail in every cafe where the fum in queftion, according to the plaintiff's account of it, amounted to £. 10, or upwards; and in no cafe was it neceffary for the plaintiff to ftate the caufe of action in the writ upon which the defendant was arrefted.

It is therefore hardly poffible to conceive any thing more completely empty, or more abfolutely falfe, than the form of writ by which, in the name of the king, his fubjects were, for want of bail, daily thrown into prifon; and yet, notwithftanding the grofs outrages againft juftice and good order, which were thus committed, in evafion of the ftatute of Henry the fixth (and which did not pafs unnoticed by the legiflature*) no preventive was thought of till the 13th of *Charles the fecond*: though during that long interval the laws of civil imprifonment had been greatly extended.

Exclufive of the fatal imperfection which has attended thefe laws from their firft extenfion over the people at large, throughout their whole progrefs, viz. their indifcriminate and unbounded operation,

---

* See 8 Eliz. c. 2. giving cofts in certain cafes to defendants vexatioufly arrefted.—Appendix Q.

there were here two manifest sources of endless abuse—1st. There was no check upon a plaintiff who was disposed, or found it convenient, to raise a groundless action for a sum beyond the credit of the defendant—And, 2d. No means were provided for informing the defendant, at the time of the arrest, for what cause he was arrested.

Although the former of these evils was more weighty than the latter, and the statute of Charles the second described both of them in very ample terms*, yet it only provided a remedy for the latter; and such a remedy as removed but part of the evil. It went no farther than to ordain, that if the certain and true cause of action was not particularly described in the writ or warrant, the defendant should only be obliged to find bail to the extent of £. 40. Whoever, therefore, was oppressively arrested upon a writ or warrant which described a special cause of action; or who could not find bail to the amount of £. 40, was as much without a remedy as ever.

What was the consequence? The *multitude* still groaned under all the evils which the statute described—the gaols were full of miserable wretches, oppressed as insolvent debtors; and the legislature expressed their regret, while they proclaimed their indolence, by inventing the feeble, and impolitic, expedient of *an act of insolvency* †.

* 13 Car. II. st. 2. c. 2.—See the description of the abuses which then prevailed, (and do still prevail) in the preamble of that statute, Appendix R.
† See chap. *infra*, upon acts of insolvency.

CHAP.

CHAP. XVI.

The Effect of the Statute of CHARLES THE SECOND *upon the Warrants of Arrest and Imprisonment of the Court of King's Bench.*

IT was formerly felt as one of the inconveniences attending those fictitious proceedings in courts of law, which were invented for such purposes as could not be avowed, that upon every alteration which the legislature found it necessary to make upon the legal course of procedure, inconsistent with actual practice, some fictitious regulations were engrafted by the courts themselves. It must ever be so. It is the object of such fictions, professedly for purposes of conveniency (which it is certain they often promote) to counteract or evade, while they *seem* to co-operate with law.

To preserve their existence, by saving appearances, those fictitious proceedings had, therefore, to accommodate themselves to whatever new shape the law might assume; and to extend or abridge their operation accordingly.

The law knew nothing of the fictitious practice by which the Court of King's Bench had acquired *an original* jurisdiction in certain civil causes; or of the summary arrest and imprisonment to which defendants, in such civil causes, were subjected by a course of process which had been calculated only for forcible injuries. The statute of Charles the second, therefore, in providing a remedy for the gross abuses it described, by ordaining that writs, &c. should specify the true cause of action, struck collaterally at the very root of that fictitious practice.

The Court of Common Pleas thought they had by this statute effectually recovered all their original jurisdiction in causes of a nature purely civil; and the officers and practitioners in the Court of King's Bench were alarmed at the prospect of losing so great and lucrative a subject of cognizance. Indeed the statute was so directly repugnant to the fiction by which they held it, that the loss appeared inevitable.

But they found relief in one of those distinctions which practical men of words* have frequently brought to bear with so much success against sense and reason. 'The statute,' it was said, 'will not be disobeyed, if what it requires is done, though *something more* shall also be done. It does, indeed, require that the true cause of action shall be specially described in the writ, but it does not say that a false cause of action may not *also* be given; therefore the statute will be obeyed, if after stating a false cause of action, viz. a fictitious trespass or forcible injury, a true cause shall also be described in the same writ. Thus the writ will have a twofold operation—the first part of it, though false,

---

* The reasonings of the courts were, even at that period, as much confined, upon many subjects, by the narrow subtleties of language, as they are now enlarged by a wise liberality of principle.

ON CIVIL IMPRISONMENT.

will, "*according to the course of the court*," found the jurisdiction—the second, being true, will comply with the law, and give notice to the defendant of the cause for which he is imprisoned *.'

In this manner the new law produced only an addition to the old fiction; and those summary warrants of imprisonment which had been formed for such trespasses as by their outrage disturbed the quiet of society, still continued to issue, upon a false suggestion, against the liberty of the peaceable trader, or unfortunate debtor.

* Accordingly the *bill of Middlesex*, or writ of *latitat* which followed it, in case the defendant was not to be found in Middlesex, from thenceforward not only required the defendant to answer as before to a plea of trespass, but contained an additional clause describing a special cause of action, thus; "And also (ac etiam) to a bill of debt, &c."—This is known by the name of the *ac etiam* clause in the bill; but it is only necessary in cases above £. 40. And in such cases an *ac etiam* clause is added to the *capias* of the Common Pleas.

CHAP.

CHAP. XVII.

The Law of Civil Imprisonment, so far as it respects the Arrest of Defendants, or, technically, Imprisonment on MESNE PROCESS, *brought down to the present Time.*

THE legiflature, in framing the ftatute of Charles the fecond, feem to have been earneftly defirous of obtaining a remedy, but not to have rightly apprehended where the ftrefs of the evil lay. The miferies they defcribed arofe more from the total want of reftraint upon the commencement of actions, by malicious or defigning plaintiffs, than the inconvenience of not informing defendants by the writ, at the time of the arreft, for what caufe they were arrefted. Yet ftill the law continued to give to plaintiffs the fame unbridled power by which, on the one hand, they might extort the hardeft advantages, as the price of peace; and on the other, had only to fear the poffible confequence of paying the cofts of the action. It was, a trade in which the hazard of lofs, was far overbalanced by the chance of gain.

Thus ftood the law, and all its attendant evils, as defcribed in the ftatute of Charles the fecond, till the reign of George the firft; when the legiflature took notice of the real fource of the mifchief; and went a certain length to cure it. A ftatute* made

* 12 Geo. I. c. 29,

ON CIVIL IMPRISONMENT.

in that reign, after enacting, for the prevention of arrests in trifling actions, that no person should be imprisoned upon any process issuing out of a superior court, where the cause of action did not amount to £. 10 or upwards; nor out of any inferior court, where the cause of action did not amount to 40 *s.* or upwards; ordains, that when the cause of action shall be of a sufficient amount to warrant the arrest of the defendant, an *affidavit* shall be made by the plaintiff of such cause of action, before a judge, or a commissioner authorized for that purpose.

In the reign of George the second this law was made perpetual.

And in the present reign*, arrests upon the *process* of inferior courts for any cause of action under the amount of £. 10 were prohibited; and all acts for the recovery of small debts, so far as they authorized the imprisonment of defendants upon process, for a cause of action under that amount, were repealed.

Thus stands the present law of arrest and imprisonment of *defendants.*

* 19 Geo. III. c. 29, § 70.—The exceptions to the general law, arising from these statutes, are stated Appendix S.

CHAP.

CHAP. XVIII.

Civil Imprisonment in Execution; or Imprisonment of DEBTORS.

IMPRISONMENT *in execution* is, technically, in contradistinction to imprisonment on *mesne process*: or, in other words, it is the imprisonment of a *debtor*, in contradistinction to the imprisonment of a *defendant*.

The power of compelling defendants to appear in the action, and that of enforcing obedience to the judgment pronounced, are the essentials of jurisdiction. If, therefore, a court can imprison the defendant during the pendency of the cause, that he may be ready to answer the event, *a fortiori* it can imprison him for the purpose of enforcing obedience to the judgment.

This seems to have been the original principle of the *capias ad satisfaciendum*; that judicial writ which issues in name of the king upon a judgment; and is directed to the sheriff, commanding him to take and safely keep the debtor, so that he may have " *his body*" in court " to satisfy" the creditor for the sum recovered, and costs adjudged.

The *capias ad satisfaciendum* is thus the warrant of imprisonment in execution. In some instances, as *in account* against bailiffs, and in *debt* [*], a capias

---
[*] 13 Edw. I. c. 11. chap. 6, supra.——25 Edw. III. c. 17 chap. 7, supra.

ON CIVIL IMPRISONMENT.

of this nature was, as we have seen, expressly given by statute. But in general it stands upon a position which, on the principle already mentioned, has long been established as law, viz. that wherever capias lies *in process*, there, after judgment, capias *ad satisfaciendum* may issue *—Or, in other words, that wherever a common law court can arrest and imprison the defendant in the action, it can imprison him as a debtor till he comply with the judgment †.

But if it happen that the debtor is insolvent, the power of the court is spent when he is so imprisoned. It has taken from him his liberty, but cannot upon circumstances restore it; and he may remain *for life* in the hands of a public officer, but in fact the prisoner of a private individual ‡.

* 3 Rep. 12. Sir William Herbert's Case.

† The limited imprisonments for small debts of 40 s. and under, by particular statute, are stated in the Appendix T.

‡ The effect of imprisonment of the *person*, in depriving the creditor of all execution against the *estate* of the debtor, during his life, is stated in the Appendix V.

The law of *Scotland*, and also the laws of foreign commercial countries, such as *Holland*, are extremely different from the law of England, respecting the imprisonment of debtors.— See Appendix U.

E PART

PART II.

CHAP. I.

The general Purpose of the following Chapters.

IF the progress and present state of those comprehensive laws of civil imprisonment which hang over the persons of all the unprivileged commons of England, have been fairly described; neither their extraction nor their aspect will procure them a favourable reception from an enlarged or benevolent mind. But it is not by the loose suggestions of general impression, or of benevolent sentiment, that laws are to be tried. They are to be justified or condemned by conclusions, deliberately drawn, from their combined effects upon the immediate happiness of the individual, and the more remote interests of the community—effects which ought reciprocally to aid or correct, by reciprocally acting upon each other.

With

With this general obfervation in view, the fubject propofed is now to be profecuted. The progrefs of the laws of civil imprifonment has been traced. It remains to ftate their immediate effects; to point out their leading qualities; to examine feparately their parts; and to confider the principles and purpofes afcribed to them—in other words, to try their operation by their object.

CHAP. II.

The immediate Effect of the Laws of Civil Imprisonment upon the Situation of the Individual — with a Reflection on the Prejudice arising from false Ideas of HUMANITY.

AN Englishman, born in that country where the fettered African becomes free; breathing liberty from his birth; and generous, from the best cause of generosity, a sense of honest independence; is struck by the hand of misfortune, rendered incapable of paying his debts, and reduced to poverty. His person is from that moment in the power of another, and his integrity affords him, in law, no possible means of relief.

Is he consigned to slavery? No. The word *slavery* is not suffered: His situation is described in milder terms: he is committed to prison, and placed under the power of his creditor, because he is unable to pay him the debt which he owes him.

How miserably are we led astray from the true nature of things by a sound!

The slave who toils in chains for his master, acts a part in society. He derives some consequence from his labour; and perhaps has never known a better state. But the imprisoned debtor, who has tasted all the sweets of liberty, must drag out his tedious hours in bondage and in idleness;

deprived,

ON CIVIL IMPRISONMENT.

deprived, perhaps for life, of all that life could enable him to enjoy.

If indeed we look into a gaol with the eye of philanthropy, a picture of human woe shall there present itself, such as imagination could never have formed. It is drawn from combinations of misery, which extend themselves far beyond the walls of the prison. They reach the sad dwelling of many a drooping family, reduced to the extremities of want, and driven perhaps to infamy——*

——There are men of no unworthy or obdurate character, who have taught their minds to take the alarm when, in the course of an argument upon a subject of general concern, pictures of private distress are presented to the feelings. They are jealous of the slightest encroachment upon what they hold to be the strict prerogatives of reason. Forgetful of the wise harmony of nature, which has ordered that no one power of the human mind can perform its due functions alone, they disable one, that another may act with better energy.

Nor is it surprising that this prejudice should often be cherished, while the weakness of those distempered feelings which disturb the judgments of men, is suffered to usurp the name of *humanity*. True humanity looks steadily upon those private miseries which are subservient to the great purposes of general happiness. Tempered by the cool

* Appendix W.

suggestions of sober reflection, it can act with determined severity; and in the pursuits of a great and extended benevolence, is superior to the influence of narrow affections.

But he who is possessed of that just humanity which *can* be severe, will feel for those who sink unheeded and unknown under the sore and unnatural pressure of perverted laws. And his judgment will approve of the feeling.—For it is wise to indulge the tenderest sympathies of the soul, when they act in unison with the best principles of justice, and the sovereign authority of public good.

CHAP.

CHAP. III.

The blind Operation of the Laws of Civil Imprisonment.

IT is rightly said that civil society must be governed by general, not by partial, rules; but it is the *principle* only that is general: the *direction* is special and relative. In municipal law, as in nature, it holds under a general principle, that different causes have different effects; that circumstances vary consequences; and yet the variation is controuled by rule.

This principle, in all its parts, would seem to be absolutely reversed by the laws of imprisonment. Let us trace their operation in a few familiar examples, beyond the line which the bankrupt laws have drawn around the trading world.

By some of those untoward accidents which cross the smoothest ways of life, or by the folly or villainy of others, a man of the purest principles and simplest manners is rendered incapable of doing justice to those who have trusted him. Reason instantly decides—he shall suffer, but yet have the benefit of his integrity; and others must partake of his misfortunes—it is the tacit condition of all our reciprocal obligations in society. But the law declares that,

that, guiltlefs as he is, he may be configned to endlefs imprifonment, by thofe whom he never meant to injure.

An innocent, nay a patriotic, projector, full of ideal improvements and. fanguine expectations; active and induftrious, but weak and vifionary; comes under engagements which he has not a doubt of being able to difcharge, but which follow the fate of his fchemes — in due courfe of law, they terminate in a gaol. He feels that he is unfortunate; but knows not how he is guilty.

A prodigal, the fport of youthful levity, and prey of fafhion; too much a coxcomb to be pofitively a villain; and yet too thoughtlefs to be truly honeft, runs heedlefs along, till he falls into the gulph which the law has prepared for him. He is taught to reflect; but may never be fuffered to profit by his experience.

And an abandoned cheat, a fmiling polifhed thief, who can command his paffions, practife fimple manners, fafcinate honour, and cajole unfufpecting honefty; whofe laborious and fyftematic profligacy has, for the ends of deliberate wickednefs, encountered and furmounted difficulties which virtue would never have known—*his* courfe at length is run—*he* has no misfortunes to lament; he cannot appeal to one honeft action; but, *as an infolvent debtor*, he meets with no harder fate than thofe who went before him.

Thus it is—By the prefent laws of imprifonment for debt, which know indeed of no diftinctions,

one

ON CIVIL IMPRISONMENT.

one common fate indiscriminately awaits the innocent and melancholy victim of misfortune; the disappointed projector; the giddy prodigal; and the abandoned profligate*.

* And such examples of injustice are, to a certain degree, unavoidable. For if the laws of imprisonment did not in their first operation proceed against debtors indiscriminately, they would seldom proceed with effect. But the fact, that such consequences are *at first* unavoidable, affords strong reason why the law should, in its common course, take notice of the situation of prisoners, and afford means for the relief of the honest, and punishment of the guilty. To shew that this is practicable, and would be politic, is the object of the following chapters: but they are not meant to go farther.—*Imprisonment for debt is indispensable.*

CHAP.

CHAP. IV.

A simple Affidavit of Debt the single preliminary Proceeding upon which a Defendant is arrested and imprisoned on the Commencement of the Action against him.

IT would be matter of novelty to many a common practioner, to be told, that for the purpose of preventing the consequences of wanton, groundless, or malicious actions, the law requires substantial security for the fair and *bonâ fide* prosecution by the plaintiff of every suit he commences in a court of justice: yet the fictitious names of *John Doe* and *Richard Roe* as pledges of prosecution, by which the practice satisfies the law, would be no novelty to his ear.

The fact is, that the sole preliminary towards the commencement of such an action as shall instantly deprive the defendant of his personal freedom is a simple *affidavit*—the oath of the plaintiff that the defendant owes him a certain sum of money. This single act of an individual, executed as a matter of course, before a person who administers an oath with the most perfect official slight and indifference, has, for the time, upon the person of him against whom the proceeding is directed, all the effect of a solemn and deliberate judgment pronounced by a supreme court of judicature.

The affidavit must be positive and direct: it must expressly aver that the defendant is indebted to

the

ON CIVIL IMPRISONMENT.

the plaintiff in a certain sum of money. This has been settled in the Court of King's Bench*, in order to counteract, if possible, by the apprehension of punishment, somewhat of the strong temptation to perjury which arises from the facility of the measure, by depriving it of the shelter which equivocal and indirect expression affords.

So much the affidavit, upon the faith of which the defendant is imprisoned, does positively state—but it is also fit to enquire what it does *not* state.

The affidavit does not state that the defendant obtained credit from the plaintiff upon false pretences.

It does not state that he is privately withdrawing his effects, for the purpose of defrauding his creditors.

It does not state that there is reason to think he is about to abscond or conceal himself.

In short, it does not state any one circumstance from which it can be inferred, or even suspected, that the defendant either has committed, or means to commit, A FRAUD, *by secreting his effects, or withdrawing his person.*

Such is the nature of the only precaution in general practice for preventing a gross abuse of legal authority, and protecting individuals from one of the worst calamities which it is in the power of one man to bring upon another †.

* Appendix X.

† There are cases where the claim being for remote and uncertain damages, the defendant cannot be arrested without a special order of the court, or of a judge, upon a special affidavit of circumstances—but the above is the general law and practice

CHAP.

CHAP. V.

The Question stated, Upon what PRINCIPLE *the Relation between Debtor and Creditor,* WITHOUT ANY CIRCUMSTANCE OF FRAUD, *draws after it the Consequence of that Imprisonment to which, by the Law as it stands, Debtors are subjected.*

WHATEVER may be the truth of the case in point of fact—whether the cause has been deliberately tried upon its merits, or the defendant has been unable to defray the cost of a defence, and has therefore despondently suffered it to take its course without interruption; it is necessarily and fairly to be inferred, after a judgment has been regularly pronounced against him by a court of justice, that he owes the debt for which he has been imprisoned. Every prisoner therefore *in execution*, that is, every person who is in prison upon a judgment, is the debtor of him at whose suit he stands so imprisoned, to the full extent of the sum contained in the judgment. No private complaint or objection, tending to the contrary, is then to be listened to: the relative situations of the two parties are fixed; the one is a just creditor, the other an insolvent debtor. But it is fair to inquire upon what *principle* it is that the relation of debtor and creditor can ever, of itself, and without the ingredient of fraud, draw after it that imprisonment to which the debtor is by law subjected.

The

ON CIVIL IMPRISONMENT.

The diſtinct and proper character of impriſonment in execution for debt, *as now practiſed*, ſeems no where to have received a correct and preciſe definition. It is to be found at one time looſely repreſented as a *puniſhment* *—at another, as a mode of *coercion* †—and at another as in itſelf a *ſatisfaction* ‡. It may alſo be conſidered by ſome as the effect of a tacit or *implied agreement* between the contracting parties; or as the means of giving effect to the juſt expectations of creditors;—and by others as matter of *public policy*.

This obſcurity which covers its principle (if, as it has long been practiſed, it has any regular principle) may be the cauſe of that blind reſpect which it has in general met with, and the ſilence in which the people at large (and a people of ſenſibility) formerly viewed even its worſt abuſes, and moſt irregular conſequences.

---

* 2 Blackſt. Com. 473.—Ibid. 3. 415.

† "The intent of the *capias ad ſatisfaciendum* is to impriſon the body of the debtor *till* ſatisfaction be made for the debt, coſts, and damages." 3 Blackſt. Com. 414.

‡ In the introduction to a very elegant panegyric upon the care and circumſpection of the law, in maintaining to every individual (among other important objects) " the enjoyment of his civil rights, without entrenching upon thoſe of any other individual in the nation," Sir William Blackſtone obſerves that the execution of a judgment " puts the party in ſpecific poſſeſſion of his right, by the intervention of miniſterial officers, or elſe *gives him an ample ſatisfaction*, either by equivalent damages, *or by the confinement of his body* who is guilty of the injury complained of."—Ibid. 422.

Here it is laid down that a creditor derives *an ample ſatisfaction* by the *confinement of the debtor's body*.

CHAP.

CHAP. VI.

Civil Imprisonment in Execution, considered as a Punishment.

IF imprisonment in execution for a civil debt is to be considered as a *punishment*, the cause of it must be a *crime:* but this will be found to involve a multitude of difficulties.

The idea of *crime* is too well understood, to require or with propriety to admit of formal definition. It is one of the simplest ideas that can be presented to the mind, and therefore shall not be made the subject of discussion.

As every insolvent debtor without any sort of distinction (except that which arises from the *bankrupt laws* in matters of trade, and what is called the *Lords Act*, both to be afterwards considered) is subjected to the possible consequence of endless imprisonment; every insolvent debtor must of course, in this view, be equally and without distinction criminal.

The character of insolvency, simply considered, arises from contracting a debt, and failing to fulfil or discharge it.

If every insolvent debtor is criminal, there must be guilt either in one or both of these circumstances, in every case where they occur.—Let the contracting of the debt be first considered.

ON CIVIL IMPRISONMENT.

In this age and country, it will hardly require argument to shew that a man commits no offence by contracting a debt which he has every *probability* in reason to think he shall have funds to discharge. But it would be an outrage against common sense any where, for a moment to suppose, that a man who has a *moral certainty* of fulfilling an engagement, does any thing amiss in coming under that engagement; only because it is within the compass of possibility that he may never be able to discharge it *.

In *contracting* the debt, therefore, which he afterwards fails to discharge, he may be perfectly innocent; because his intentions may be fair, and his prospects just and rational.

And *in failing to discharge* the debt he has contracted, he may be equally innocent; for that may happen in as many different ways as there are varieties in the unforeseen events of life.

If this be so, it cannot surely be said, that while each of the two ingredients is consistent with perfect integrity and innocence †, *the law* shall hold at the same time that there is guilt in the general character of insolvent debtor, which is composed of both; that it began by his contracting the debt, and was consummated by his failing to discharge it; and that, by one more of those fictions which sometimes elude the grasp of reason, amidst the subtleties of artificial system, the legal offence of failing to pay, by *relating back* to the contraction of the debt, taints the whole from beginning to

* See *Puffendorff* and *Barbeyrac*, Appendix Y.
† Appendix Z.

end,

end, and raises up a criminal in the eye of law, without the aid either of criminal act or intention—propositions there certainly are which are formed of no better materials.

But even when it happens that an insolvent debtor is not thus converted into a criminal by operation of law, without any consciousness or interposition of his own; but is truly guilty of fraud, either by contracting the debt, without any view to the means of payment, or by not afterwards applying the means in his power towards discharging it; and that, in common with others, he is imprisoned, perhaps for life; he is so imprisoned, not as a person who has been guilty of fraud, but simply as an insolvent debtor. The real truth of the case could never be discovered from this its legal consequence. Even the gaoler cannot, from appearances, distinguish a prisoner of the former description from one of the latter; if it be not perchance by the levity of the one, and the despondency of the other—the former, relieved by a situation milder than he knew he deserved; the latter, depressed by a state of misery which he never did any thing to deserve.

If insolvency, as being often consistent with the fairest intentions, cannot *in itself* be criminal; imprisonment in execution, for civil debt, cannot be rendered consistent with the idea of punishment.

But there are other reasons why that sort of imprisonment cannot be reconciled to the principles of punishment.

The punishment of crimes or offences is a matter of public concern, and inflicted by the public.

Punishment

ON CIVIL IMPRISONMENT.

Punishment is also proportioned to the guilt of the offender: when, therefore, the guilt admits of distinctions and degrees, so does the punishment.

But imprisonment in execution is inflicted by one individual upon another, who therefore suffers privately, at the pleasure of a fellow citizen, without the knowledge, attention, or interference of the public: and although his insolvency, if at all to be considered as criminal, must admit of various degrees and modifications, the law prescribes no limits to the possible endurance of his sufferings. As an insolvent debtor he may be innocent, and his creditor permitted to torment him;—as an insolvent debtor he may be criminal, and his creditor suffered, from the impulse of the moment, to turn him loose and unpunished upon society.

Punishment is not to avenge, but to warn and instruct. There is a grandeur in public principle which disdains the little objects of passion. But imprisonment in execution, while it gratifies private vengeance, and may ruin the person who suffers it, can never operate by way of example for the good of others. The reason is most manifest; it falls from no height; it is the blow of an equal, perhaps of an avowed enemy; it provokes resentment or indignation; it is indiscriminate and capricious in its application—it is consequently uncertain and impotent.

A mind so constructed, or formed by mean habits, as to act chiefly from the fear of punishment, will also be industrious and cunning in discovering means to elude it; and where there is so much

much uncertainty, there never can be any fixed apprehenfion.

Moreover, if imprifonment in execution for a civil debt is a punifhment, it is a punifhment of which the feverity may often rife in exact proportion to the innocence and worth of the fufferer. The depraved and grovelling foul of a villain can find enjoyments in a gaol—it is the weak, but generous dupe of artifice, or the prey of misfortune, who feels all its horrors*.

* Appendix A A.

CHAP. VII.

Civil Imprisonment in Execution considered as a Mode of COERCION.

IT has been held, and seems indeed, from the terms of the writ or warrant, to have been the original idea of the law, that civil imprisonment in execution is merely a mode of *coercion*, or an imprisonment till satisfaction be made—that is, until a dishonest man is compelled, *squalore carceris*, to do justice.

Then what is to be said for it when it acts against an honest man, for the purpose of compelling him to perform an impossibility? The same thing which has been said for *torture* when inflicted upon innocence, as the *possible* means of, sometimes, extorting a discovery of guilt.

The law, it is said, presumes that every man is able to perform the promise or engagement he has made; and concludes that his failure is therefore wilful. And this is right—but the law goes farther. The *prima facie* evidence of a legal presumption is made to change its nature; and instead of being open to contrary evidence, is held to be absolute and conclusive: for the debtor has no possible means of proving his innocence and inability.

Imprifonment therefore for debt, in the prefent ftate of the law, if it acts as a mode of coercion, acts with the certainty of often offending againft juftice, and only the chance of fometimes promoting it.

CHAP.

CHAP. VIII.

Civil Imprisonment in Execution considered as in itself a Legal SATISFACTION *to the Creditor.*

THERE are not only many sayings of lawyers, but also established legal distinctions, which represent imprisonment for debt as being *in itself a satisfaction* to the creditor. Considering it in this light, we shall be no less unsuccesful in our inquiries for something consistent or rational in its nature.

A legal satisfaction must be something received in return for something given—Let this be applied—A creditor has of his own accord, and with the circumstances, to which he trusted, open to inquiry, lent his money, or sold his goods. In general he can only be repaid by money or goods. Yet the law does not lead the creditor first to inquire after his debtor's money or goods to which he trusted; but says, he may instantly proceed to recover a satisfaction, not by receiving any thing himself, but by depriving his debtor of his personal freedom. For that purpose it arms him with the power of delivering over the body of his debtor into the custody of other men, whose duty it is to deprive him of the common air of heaven, and reduce him to the lowest state of animal existence.

A legal

A legal satisfaction, whether real or fictitious, can, without a contradiction in terms, be considered in no other light than as a legal equivalent. How is it, then, that the perpetual imprisonment of a fellow citizen is, in the eye of law, no more than a satisfaction for twenty pounds, and yet is also a satisfaction for twenty thousand?

A satisfaction admits of gradation; it may be in part or in full: but imprisonment for an hour has the same value in law as imprisonment for life. *If the debtor has once entered the walls of a prison as a debtor in execution, the creditor loses from that moment every substantial means of enforcing payment during his debtor's life.* The debtor may possess the wealth of the Indies—if he is contented to possess it in a gaol, (a secure and well-accommodated retreat for the enjoyments of avarice) he may laugh at the idle anger of his creditor, and dare him to touch his manors or his coffers *.

If the satisfaction which arises *in law* to the creditor from the imprisonment of his debtor, proceeds upon the idea that the debtor is made to suffer in one way for what the creditor suffers in another, the matter will be found equally inextricable. A debtor who is honest and unfortunate; who feels that high relish for freedom and independence, which is the chief felicity of worthy minds; who has hitherto perhaps enjoyed the best blessings of domestic life, and the innocent pleasures of society, suffers infinitely more by the loss of his liberty, than he who never knew how to use, and for ever abused, the

* Appendix B.B.

means

ON CIVIL IMPRISONMENT.

means of happiness—but the debt of the latter may be infinitely greater than that of the former. Considering then the imprisonment of the debtor as in itself a satisfaction, of the nature described, the reasoning (if it deserve the name) terminates in this; that the loss of the creditor may be trivial, and his debtor rendered miserable; or his loss may be great; and his debtor hardly affected.

When we read the criminal laws of certain nations in a rude state of society, we find every member of the human body, as well as life itself, had its legal valuation in money. We are struck at the brutality of men who could thus coolly and deliberately, at the table of state, form, with minute and barbarous precision, a scale of compositions; according to which a man had only to count his money, in order to know how he could best afford to gratify the rage of a savage—whether by breaking the bones, or beating out the brains, of his enemy.

In England we dare not shed the blood of our neighbours; we cannot deprive them of their limbs, or of their lives; but, at a certain expence, we can effectually disable them from enjoying the use of them. Under the mask of friendship, a man may tempt the destined victim of his cruelty to become his debtor: he may practise on his failings, and encourage his follies; he may then deprive him legally of his liberty, and consign him to misery. For £.20 he can take from under the orders of the king the person of a soldier in the immediate service of his country: for £.20 he can lock up the body of an able seaman, when men must be hunted down to support the honour and safety of the nation: for 2*s.* 4*d.* a week*, or £. 5. 11*s.* 4*d.* a year, he can hold a fellow citizen in perpetual durance—so that for little more than £. 100 a year, a man, in this land of freedom, may purchafe the bondage of twenty wretched prifoners. It is enough to fay that this is *poffible*, and would be no more than the exercife of a legal right.

The queftion may now be afked, Which of the two, the *criminal* code of the antient Germans, or this branch of the *civil* laws of England, is the moft barbarous?

If it is true (for the idea would feem to have arifen from the mifapprehenfion of a figurative expreffion †) that the Romans ever received it as a law that creditors might cut their debtors in pieces, an example of mad ferocity in legiflation is there afforded, which aftonifhes reafon, and fhocks humanity. But thofe early laws of the moft polifhed ftate in *Greece* (afterwards reformed by *Solon*) and of other nations, by which infolvent debtors, and even fometimes their wives and children, were ufed or fold by their creditors as flaves; or the law of *Ruffia*, by which a Mufcovite is delivered over to his creditor, firft to be well beaten by him, and then made his flave; have nothing in them fo *irrational*, at leaft, as the Englifh law of civil imprifonment. For fuch laws are not both cruel and inefficient; they do not take every thing from the debtor, and yet give nothing to the creditor ‡.

* This is the fubfiftence allowed under the *Lords Act*, to be afterwards explained.

† Appendix C C.   ‡ Appendix D D.

CHAP.

CHAP. IX.

Civil Imprisonment considered upon the Principle of an implied or tacit Agreement.

WHEN system has lost sight of the simplicity of nature, and is pushed to the extreme of resorting upon every occasion to artificial principle, it confounds, instead of aiding, the reasonings of men. The mind is made to wander by a circuitous progress, through laboured and forced implications, in search of an object which lay directly before it; and the plainest truths are obscured by the intricacies of abstract demonstration.

The strength and energy of those principles of law and of equity, which are to be met with throughout all the different parts of *Roman* jurisprudence, have furnished rules and maxims of municipal law to every nation in Europe. But *some* of the theories which rose upon the principles of that great and justly celebrated system were much too refined for practical application. They gave employment to commentators; but could never reach the understandings of the people. Nor was it necessary they should—they were the mere play of words; or the combination of fanciful ideas, which had seldom any ultimate effect upon the subject. From the same facts the same conclusion would have been drawn by the clown, and by the lawyer. Both would have agreed,

agreed, for example, that if a man received money which had been paid by miftake, and which was not due to him, he was bound to reftore it. But their reafons would have founded very differently. The former felt fimply the obligation of natural juftice—the latter had been taught the legal effect of a covenant *in law*, which never exifted *in fact*; and could demonftrate, upon a multitude of authorities, the binding force of *tacit* agreements, and the legal import of that *quafi contractus* which arofe *ex indebiti folutione**. Accuftomed to the idea of pofitive obligation, as being the confequence of exprefs agreement, the Roman lawyers carried the fame *form* of reafoning through the whole chain of duties which were inherent in the nature of things, and imprinted on the mind of every upright man. They fuppofed a contract, and inferred an obligation. They proved by falfe fuggeftions, what in itfelf was moft manifeftly true.

We have had occafion to obferve that no fmall portion of the fame fpirit of unneceffary fubtlety and refinement (though affecting more the management of *forms*, than of abftract principles, and derived in moft inftances from a different origin) is to be found in many of the theories of law in this country. If fo, it is not impoffible that the imprifonment of an infolvent debtor may be reprefented as the fair refult of public law, giving effect to a *tacit* agreement or

---

* In the fame manner they accounted fcientifically for obligations equally apparent, arifing *ex negotiorum geftione, tutela; rei communione, aditione haereditatis*, and the like. Appendix EE.

quafi

ON CIVIL IMPRISONMENT.

quasi contract between the parties; the creditor, it may be said, trusting to that legal consequence; the debtor agreeing to submit to it if he fail in the fulfilment of his engagement.

This would indeed be reasoning in a circle; but it will not be difficult to shew, upon other grounds, that the law of civil imprisonment can derive no aid from any such argument.

By one of those honourable restraints which the genius of civil liberty puts upon the actions of men, no possible mode of bargain, transaction, or covenant, can place two individuals in the relation to each other of master and slave: for every subject of a free government is a *citizen:* a character which may be forfeited by crime, but cannot be surrendered by contract.

Under such a government, individuals are taught to feel their importance by the immediate dependance of the public upon their exertions towards the general welfare. No middle power is interposed between them and the state. The blessings of public prosperity are not intercepted by a subordinate tyrant in their way to the cottage of the labourer. He feels their immediate effects, and can indulge the honest pride of having contributed directly towards them. In such a state it is, that public and private good are, in truth, co-existent and reciprocal: in others, they are only so in speculation.

But this vivifying quality of liberty; this mutual energy, which is for ever acting upon the individuals which compose the community of a free state; would speedily be lost, if under the necessity of the

moment

moment men were permitted to surrender their power of contributing, independently, and in their own proper persons, to the public service. Incapable of promoting, they would feel no right to enjoy their country's welfare. The interest of the public would be no longer theirs. It would be their masters'.

It is the constitutional boast of Englishmen, that the public good is an estate in common; of the free possession and enjoyment of which no law can deprive the humblest individual who is not convicted of a crime.

What multitudes then there are who are bereft of their civil existence by the laws of imprisonment! But is it possible to maintain that those laws have proceeded upon this solecism in the language of freedom; that a community can be truly free, while individuals may, by their own consent, be slaves?

Personal dependence, and the want of those civil rights which others enjoy, form the essence of slavery. Substantially they are lost to him who is rendered incapable of enjoying them: and such is the state of the prisoner for debt.

In letting out his labour to hire, no man loses a particle of his civil liberty. He is at that moment spontaneously contributing to the general good. He is upon a footing with his employer: he gives in one way, and receives in another.

Would it be so with a man who stipulated that, in a certain event, his neighbour should be entitled to

deprive

ON CIVIL IMPRISONMENT. 77

deprive him of the use of his limbs; or that if he failed to pay a sum of money, his person should be locked up *in idleness,* and his existence rendered equally insignificant to himself and to the public? —Would this be a lawful contract?

CHAP.

CHAP. X.

Civil Imprisonment considered with a View to the established legal Presumption of fair Intention, 'till the Contrary is proved.

WHATEVER may be inferred to the contrary from the principles of certain doctrines, it will in general be found, that the reasonings of law, in the establishment of legal presumptions, are full of candour and liberality; proceeding upon maxims favourable to the characters of men, and excluding the idea of unfair or unjust intentions, till the contrary is established by evidence.

It is thus that it presumes respecting the views of a creditor when he gives credit. In transacting with the debtor, he is presumed to have looked no farther than to that which was fairly before him, viz. the ability of the debtor himself, by means either of present effects or *probable* acquirements, to discharge the debt: and, conformably to this presumption, whatever may tend to hang out false colours, that is, to give false appearances, and lead to credit, where there is not substance, is upon every occasion reprobated by the law.

The law of imprisonment, however, is inconsistent with this presumption; or makes use of it with partiality: it admits it on one side, and rejects it on the other.

It is manifest that there must be something wrong on one side or the other, when, in the common course of affairs, a man gives his property, upon a promise of something equivalent, to one who has neither property to support his promise, nor the *probable* means of acquiring it. Either the person who gives the credit has some malignant design against the man himself who receives it, or some rapacious view towards inordinate gain; or he who receives it has obtained it by falsehood and deceit.

In every case; without inquiry; by mere presumption, the law imputes the whole to the latter; and yet it inflicts no public punishment upon him. As to the conduct of him who gave the credit, no notice whatever is taken of it. In every case; without inquiry; upon mere presumption, HE is viewed as an injured man*.

If considerations different from those which arise, *bonâ fide*, from the apparent ability of the debtor, either by present means or *probable* acquirement, have weighed in the mind of the creditor; they may be such as the law ought not perhaps to reprobate; but they cannot be such as the law ought actively to support. If he knew that his debtor had neither funds nor effects, and yet chose to trust to accident; that is, to run the hazard of loss, rather than forego the chance of gain, he cannot justly apply to the law for its interposition, if the event is unfavourable; because it was directly under his view at the time of

---

* Some of the points here generally stated, are more fully considered in subsequent chapters.

the

the tranfaction, and he had knowingly made a bargain of hazard. Or if, apprifed that he never could be paid by the debtor himfelf, he trufted to the fecret expectation that the debtor's *friends* would be induced, from motives of benevolence, to fubject themfelves to the lofs, rather than fuffer him to go to gaol, the expectation was both unjuft and illegal; unjuft, becaufe it went beyond the terms of the bargain, which proceeded fingly upon the credit of the debtor himfeif; illegal, as having been inconfiftent with the principle that the province of law is not to create new fecurities, but to render effectual thofe which have been given—not to enlarge, but to carry into effect the agreements of parties *.

* In the cafe of *Smith v. Bromley*, Lord Mansfield, reprobating the iniquity of a creditor, in having taken money from the fifter of his debtor for figning his certificate as a bankrupt, or, in other words, for agreeing not to put him in prifon, expreffes himfelf thus: " If any near relation is induced to pay " the money for the bankrupt, it is taking an unfair advantage, " and torturing the compaffion of his family."—*Douglas*, 696.

The reader need hardly be reminded, that the obfervations which have been made refpecting the *principle* of civil imprifonment, refer to the common cafe, where direct *fraud*, or deception, has not been alledged againft the debtor; and where he is not only willing to give up his effects to his creditors, but ready to fubmit his conduct to the clofeft infpection.

CHAP.

CHAP. XI.

The Deference justly due to Reasons of POLICY, *or general Utility, upon this Subject.*

SUPPOSING it to have been shewn that the law of civil imprisonment, in its utmost extent, as now practised, can be referred to no regular principle: that it acts neither as a punishment: nor as a mode of coercion: nor as a satisfaction: nor as the result of an implied agreement, or legal presumption: still it is to be supported, if it can be shewn, that whatever may be its nature; however untenable it may appear in argument or speculation; its effects must, upon the whole, be salutary and conducive to the general good: and much more so if it can be shewn, that it is *necessary* for the prevention of general mischief. If again the very reverse of these propositions shall be made out, it cannot stand, whatever may be its principle.

Let the question therefore be now tried and decided upon that issue.

CHAP. XII.

Reasons of POLICY *against the present Law of Civil Imprisonment, founded upon the Authority of the* BANKRUPT LAWS.

AS the imprisonment of the person of a debtor, who had committed no forcible injury or palpable fraud, was first introduced in favour of a particular body of men, for the purpose of promoting the interest of trade; so it has received its first check for the purpose of promoting the same end. The principle was the same in both instances; but it was the same principle, acting upon the different circumstances of far different times.

The privilege given to merchants (and wisely so given) in the reign of *Edward the third*, of arresting and imprisoning their debtors for debts contracted in trade, soon recoiled, by its abuse, upon the merchants themselves; who were no sooner seen to bend under a casual loss, than they were immediately thrown down by imprisonment, at the suit of competitors. Their effects were torn to pieces by those who could first reach them; and their persons became useless matter in prison.

By a variety of statutes commencing in the reign of *Henry the eighth*, and brought down to the present times, certain acts and circumstances are described and ascertained, as legal symptoms of a situation

ON CIVIL IMPRISONMENT.

situation inconsistent with the fair capacity of trading. The person in such circumstances, if a trader, is to be declared a *bankrupt*—that is, his transactions in trade are instantly to stop; his powers of acting are for a time to cease; his affairs from that moment to become stationary; and his course of life, in the world of business, again to commence anew.

Nothing can carry along with it, upon a general view of its principle, more striking marks of strong sense and sound policy.

But it was not till the reign of Queen Anne that a bankrupt, who had done every thing in his power towards the satisfaction of his creditors, was in any degree protected from the laws of imprisonment. Till then the bankrupt's person was at the mercy of his creditors; and the caprice or resentment of any one of them, might deprive his country of the industry of an intelligent trader[*].

[*] By the 5th of George the second, c. 30, upon a certificate signed first by four-fifths of the creditors in number and value, and then by the commissioners of bankrupt, purporting, that the bankrupt has conformed himself to the law, and made a fair surrender; if that certificate be allowed by the lord chancellor, he is free and discharged for ever from all debts owing by him at the time he became bankrupt; and if he is in prison for such debts, he obtains his liberty.

The first act of parliament giving the benefit of certificate was 4 & 5 Anne, c. 17; and by that act the *commissioners* of bankrupt *only* were to sign it. The 5 Anne, c. 22, added the *creditors*—and so the law was continued, or revived (with some interruption) till the above statute, 5 Geo. the second, put the subject of certificate upon its present footing.

Lord *Hardwick* somewhere says, that the first act of Q. Anne giving bankrupts the benefit of certificate, was intended as a temporary provision, on account of the losses sustained by our trade in the succession war.

That this defect in laws of such liberal operation should have continued the greatest part of two centuries of these our later times, will cease to be matter of wonder, when it is considered that the general law respecting every unprivileged individual in the kingdom, still labours under the same sort of defect in its fullest extent.

The bankrupt laws as they now stand, however imperfect they may, in certain respects, be thought by some, are perhaps, *upon the whole,* a fit subject of panegyric: and they have been so treated by that elegant commentator, who, in displaying the outlines, and enlarging upon the leading points of English jurisprudence, has presented so pleasing a picture to the general view of the people. He has expressed himself as follows: " Trade cannot be
" carried on without mutual credit on both sides:
" the contracting of debts is therefore here not
" only justifiable, but necessary. And if by acci-
" dental calamities, as by the loss of a ship in a
" tempest, the failure of brother traders, or by the
" non-payment of persons out of trade, a mer-
" chant, or trader, becomes incapable of dis-
" charging his own debts, it is his misfortune
" and not his fault. To the misfortunes therefore
" of debtors the law has given a compassionate
" remedy, but denied it to their faults; since
" at the same time that it provides for the se-
" curity of commerce, by enacting, that every
" considerable trader may be declared a bankrupt
" for the benefit of his creditors as well as himself;
" it has also, to discourage extravagance, declared,
" that

" that no one shall be capable of being made a
" bankrupt, but only a *trader*, nor capable of re-
" ceiving the full benefit of the statutes but only
" an *industrious* trader*." And after mentioning,
that the bankrupt is protected from the law of imprisonment, he sums up its just and beneficial effects
as follows; " Thus the bankrupt becomes a clear
" man again; and, by the assistance of his allow-
" ance, and his own industry, may become a use-
" ful member of the commonwealth; which is the
" rather to be expected, as he cannot be entitled
" to these benefits, but by the testimony of his cre-
" ditors themselves of his honest and ingenuous
" disposition; and unless his failures have been
" owing to misfortunes, rather than to misconduct
" and extravagance †."

That the bankrupt laws ought to be extended to *all* honest insolvent debtors, without variation or distinction, is not to be urged. They are in many respects inapplicable to the circumstances of other descriptions of men. The machine is too great and costly for the flight and minute materials upon which in that case it would have frequently to act. Besides, the great end for which it was constructed is to arrest for a time the active powers of men, who, in struggling against a tide to which they ought patiently to give way, are not only wasting their own strength in vain, but also endangering others.

* 2 Blackst. Com. 474, Appendix F F.
† Ibid. 484.

But does it follow, that therefore no part of the *spirit* of these laws should be extended to other descriptions of men? They provide " against the inhumanity of the creditor, who is not suffered to confine an honest bankrupt after his effects are delivered up; at the same time taking care that all his just debts shall be paid, so far as the effects will extend." They have, for the declared objects of their protection, those persons who are " liable to accidental losses, and to an inability of paying their debts without any fault of their own," making them " clear men again, in order that they may become useful members of the commonwealth." In short, " they give to the misfortunes of debtors a compassionate remedy, but deny it to their faults.".

This is the language of the bankrupt laws. But does it not apply to every *honest* insolvent debtor? The answer generally given is in the negative; and the reasons have been quoted. Let them now be examined.

1. " *Trade cannot be carried on without mutual credit on both sides*."—But as the world is now situated, in the midst of that infinite variety of mutual and reciprocal dependencies which render the whole line of things but one continued chain, can *any* of the affairs of men be carried on without *mutual credit*?—Most certainly no.—Shall the husbandman sit idle till the price of his crops becomes due? or the artist desist from the prosecution of useful improvements and discoveries, and work as a labourer, rather

ON CIVIL IMPRISONMENT.

rather than borrow the means of prefent fupport from thofe who are willing to truft to his future ability? Muft the landed man convert his acres into gold; receive his rents in weekly payments; or decline the offer of a valuable purchafe rather than contract a *reafonable* debt? Or is the monied man to keep his coin in his ftrong box; and, like the *Don Bernard* of Gil Blas, to count out with daily care the price of his daily fubfiftence?

2. In trade "*the contracting of debts is not only juftifiable, but neceffary*"—it is certainly fo—but where is the fituation in which the fair contraction of a debt, with a certain or *rational* profpect of having the means of repayment, requires a juftification?

3. "*If by accidental calamities, as by the lofs of a fhip in a tempeft, the failure of brother traders, or by the non-payment of perfons out of trade, a merchant or trader becomes incapable of difcharging his own debt, it is his misfortune, and not his fault.*" Thefe circumftances are faid to furnifh the principle upon which the relief given to infolvent debtors under the bankrupt laws can be extended to traders only; but if thefe circumftances are either ideal, or not peculiar to traders, they cannot fupport the diftinction.

That a trader may fuffer a *fatal* calamity by the lofs of a fhip in a tempeft, is a fact juft within the compafs of poffibility; but neither with refpect to the prefent time, nor to the time at which the conditional protection in queftion was firft afforded to traders, can the fuppofition go farther. There was a time, a time, it is true, when the whole fortune of a merchant might have been fcattered by the winds of heaven and irrecoverably loft: but now he can fleep in quiet. He may be deprived of a profit, or fuftain a partial lofs, but the divifion of hazard by *infurance* muft, with common prudence, protect him from any *fatal* calamity.

The other calamities which have been ftated as peculiar to traders are " *the failure of brother traders,* " *or the non-payment of perfons out of trade.*"

If thefe are truly peculiar to traders; if none but traders do in fact fuffer by the failure of traders, or of perfons out of trade, it is fit that none but traders fhould have any remedy againft the indifcriminate feverity and injuftice of the laws of imprifonment. But if there are no fuch peculiarities, it follows, that a principle which the legiflature has acknowledged to be wife, as well as juft and humane, fhould be extended and adapted, by proper qualification, to the unhappy circumftances of others in a fimilar fituation *.

If we do but look into the world as it truly is, we fhall fee, that men of all defcriptions are liable to the preffure of fuch remote and unforefeen calamities, as arife from the neceffary action and reaction of *credit*; that every man muft in one form or another avail himfelf of it; that it is in fact the cement which binds together the feveral materials of an advanced fociety, and gives force and energy to the whole.

* Appendix G G.

But

ON CIVIL IMPRISONMENT.

But in enquiring how far this principle may be the subject of regulation by municipal law, its general nature, and some of the circumstances which attend it, ought to be particularly considered.

CHAP. XIII.

Thoughts on the proper Influence of Municipal Law, over the selfish Propensities of private Individuals; and on the general Nature and Circumstances of CREDIT—*introductory to certain other Reasons of* POLICY *against the Laws of Civil Imprisonment.*

IT is the perfection of legislative wisdom to derive ingredients, for the general good, from the selfish propensities of individuals. Vices are to be corrected, but selfish propensities are only to be regulated: the former, by direct; the latter by indirect means. Both must vary with the ever varying course of things. But the laws of a free, and still more of a commercial country, will, at all times, and in all circumstances, leave every man the master of his own conduct, where it encroaches upon none of the legal rights of his neighbour—for it is in the fluctuation of that rapid and irregular tide which the use, abuse, or neglect of circumstances creates, that indolence or incapacity sinks into insignificance, and merit is carried forward to the superiority it deserves. *There* the laws will neither dictate nor command: a spirit of opposition or of evasion would rise up to defeat them. But they will instigate or dissuade. They will insensibly lead the individual to choose, of his own accord, and for his own private purposes, that course, which,

with

with his own, may most promote the good of others.

In the rudest state of society men are only stimulated to exertion by the immediate impulse of appetite: their activity is violence; and their indolence, stupidity. In such a state, that covetousness which is inherent in human nature leads to rapine. By the hand of cultivation, the same spirit is meliorated into the principle of industry. Refinements are devised in the supply of reciprocal wants. The simple barter of goods for goods, gives way to the immediate delivery of goods by him who has them to dispose of, for the promise of greater value in return, at a future day, by him who has them not at present. Present wants are thus supplied by means not only of present superfluity, but also of future acquisition. The mercantile system is founded; and the progress of social happiness rapidly accelerated.

That confidence which thus communicates the possessions, while it encreases the enjoyments of the individual, and diffuses vigour through the community, by directing the self-interest of each to the good of all, receives, emphatically, the appellation of CREDIT.

Such is the general nature of the principle which now pervades almost all the transactions of society—in itself sufficiently well understood; but, in some of its circumstances, the subject of much prejudice, of some difficulty, and of weighty importance.

As it collects upon one point the full force, not only of the means which we possess at present,

but

but also of those which stand within the compass of reasonable expectation, its powers are immense. Hence its vast utility when it acts under the direction of that judgment, which can rightly estimate the value of the passing occasion.

Nor is it *necessarily* productive of general bad consequence when misapplied. If one man shall sustain a loss, another may thereby reap a fair advantage, and the *equilibrium* is preserved.

But that equilibrium, which the natural vibrations of credit have the effect to preserve, may be destroyed by the LAW.

There is therefore a time when it is the part of the legislature to encourage and promote the operations of credit in the hands of industry; as there is also a time, when, if they ought not to be restrained, they are not at least to be forced beyond their natural bounds, by extraordinary favour, or public privilege. The lax and feeble powers of infancy, or the infirmities of old age, may sometimes stand in need of aids, which would be destruction to manhood in its middle stage. A skilful physician will beware of ever correcting by medicine, what nature herself can throw off. Her salutary exertions are not to be so disturbed. The fever of physic would ensue; and the symptoms of the original disease be confounded with those of the intended remedy.

CHAP.

CHAP. XIV.

The same Subject continued.

THAT vice of the mind, which bears the appellation of *hoarding avarice*, is doubtless of pernicious consequence to society. But the evils it creates are of the negative sort. The individual is reduced to a state of insignificance; and loses all the best faculties of nature. In himself therefore he is more an object of compassion than of resentment; and we only smile at his preposterous folly. The injury he does to society consists in his withholding the means of industry and happiness: he does no positive harm, and must be left the prey of his own wretchedness.

But there is a species of avarice which is of an active quality. It springs up and thrives only in commercial states, and all the mischiefs it creates are positive and direct. It arises from the same disease in the mind which leads to hoarding avarice; acting only upon a different character, and in different circumstances—the same disposition to engross the goods of life, to the exclusion of our neighbour, affords the motive. But it deceives the world, because it bears a respected name. It is industry; but industry become morbid and excessive.

The

The trader, who acts under the impulse of this restless and rapacious spirit, may frequently bring ruin upon himself, but must with certainty bring it upon others. On the one hand, by the arts of monopoly, he cuts off those wholesome springs which circulate the blessings of real and substantial industry. On the other, with a view to inordinate gain, he spreads far and wide the goods he has engrossed, by holding forth to the adventurer, in the lower orders of trade, all the temptations of extraordinary credit and confidence. The needy adventurer in his turn, with a blind and fatal activity, exchanges his goods for the mere name of every moneyless prodigal; and the prodigal, allured by the same facility of credit, is encouraged to take a share in the common mischief, by contracting debts which he never can discharge.

Thus it happens that in the whole course of the circle, the substance or property of the person contracting the debt, may never once have been the subject of enquiry.

If any delusion, held forth by the law, tends to promote the course, or obstruct the natural corrective of these errors, it calls for the animadversion of the people.

CHAP.

CHAP. XV.

Reasons of POLICY *against these Laws, as rather tending to encourage, than restrain, an* EXCESSIVE FACILITY OF CREDIT, *and the Progress of Extravagance.*

IT is for the generous character of candid and unsuspecting good faith, that the *British* merchant is justly renowned over the world. But every virtue has its neighbouring vice. It is the lot of humanity. The covetous principles of monopoly, and of mercantile avarice, follow hard upon the right spirit of enterprize; and a blameable looseness of transaction is too frequently the effect of an unsuspecting liberality.

Unfortunately it requires no argument to prove, that a *forced and fictitious trade*, rising out of an inordinate spirit of speculation, has become a great and growing evil in the commercial world. Those bands of desperate adventurers, who float in air, afford too many proofs of its existence. The selfish propensity which leads to it cannot with safety be restrained; but the *means* by which it acts, and which are of its own formation, *ought not at least to be aided by the laws.*

It acts by means of a general and extreme FACILITY OF CREDIT*.

If there is any truth in what has been before advanced, this extreme facility of credit proceeds, at least as much from him who gives, as from him who receives it. To extend beyond all bounds their several lines of trade may be the object of both, if both are traders; but as traders deal with persons who are not in trade, it must often be the object of him only who gives the credit. Yet it seems hitherto to have been understood that the laws, in restraining that excess in the operation of credit, by deterring from its abuse, take notice only of him who receives, not of him who *gives* the credit.

In other words, with an object of public magnitude and immediate general concern before them, the laws have confined their view to a matter of private manners, affecting only the individual; namely, the prevention of private extravagance—a thing beyond the power of direct and positive law, without the tyranny of sumptuary regulations.

The laws of civil imprisonment, it has been said, severe, indiscriminate, disproportioned, and unprincipled as they may otherwise be, are just and wise upon the whole, because they tend to prevent all those miseries which extravagance, and the ease of obtaining credit, if unrestrained by the terrors of

---

* This expression is made use of to prevent circumlocution; and denotes not only the ease with which credit is obtained, *but also the fatal rashness with which it is given.*

these

ON CIVIL IMPRISONMENT.

these laws, would unavoidably produce. Let this idea be analysed.

A man who is about to contract a debt, which he cannot discharge, is checked, it is said, by the reflection that he may be thrown into gaol by his creditor.

Let it be supposed that a prodigal thus reasons upon the possible consequences of things, and even that they act upon his mind as they would upon the mind of him who makes the supposition. Then one man, it must be confessed, is thereby dissuaded from *taking* credit: but is not another, by the selfsame means, encouraged to *give* it?

It is not enough to consider the reflections which may possibly arise in the mind of a man who is about to become a *debtor*. It is necessary to give equal weight to the reflections of one who is about to become a *creditor*. A person offers him a considerable order in the line of his business—he has just heard of him, and knows where he resides.*—He hesitates, but is soon resolved—" This order," says he, " will be lucrative, and the man will pay " me rather than go to gaol." His mind is satisfied. The idea of his power, as a creditor, over the *person* of his debtor, co-operates with a spirit of industry, already too keen, and leads him astray from the substantial inquiry he might otherwise have

---

* Or perhaps the same man may have before given him an order for some trifling articles, and punctually paid him—for this is a common artifice.

H made.

made. He gives the credit: the day of payment arrives; the debtor fails—the creditor then fees the delufion to which he trufted; he is difappointed and provoked—he vents his anger according to law; drags his debtor to prifon; and purchafes peace to his refentment, by the merited, but unavailing, diftrefs he inflicts.

If thefe oppofite effects of the laws of imprifonment upon credit, reftraining one man from taking it, while they encourage another to give it, are even *equal*, the argument in fupport of their *policy* is deftroyed. But they are not equal. How are the parties defcribed, by thofe who maintain that the laws of imprifonment are a check upon extravagance? One of them as a man of bufinefs, cool, collected and deliberate; weighing confequences, and judging of the ideas of others by his own. The other a prodigal, carelefs, diffipated, and extravagant—of courfe inattentive to the view of future confequences. It is impoffible that any impreffion, arifing from reflection, can ever operate, with equal force, upon fuch oppofite characters.

Are then the prefent laws of civil imprifonment wife, in putting a check upon the improvident; when it is the improvident only who never think of them?

Are they wife, in affording a motive, which may accelerate the courfe (already much too rapid) of a loofe and unguarded credit?

Or

Or are they wife, in holding forth to the creditor's view an illufory and fictitious fatisfaction; and thereby diverting his attention from that which ought to have been the fubftantial object of his inquiry?

CHAP. XVI.

Reasons of Policy against these Laws, as affording Temptations to the Commission of Extortion and Fraud; by affording the ready Means of Oppression.

BY means even of those imperfect lights, which, in matters of practice, professional books afford, many avenues to fraud and oppression may be clearly discerned among the laws of civil imprisonment; and some of them have been already pointed out. But he who wishes to see the true extent of such abuses, must leave his library, and look abroad into the world.

The growth of dishonesty, when once it takes root among the lower orders of men, is incredibly rapid; and nothing is more certain, than that those who have themselves been bruised by oppression, become often the most unrelenting oppressors. Many a miserable man there is, who was honest till he was ruined by injustice. Having surrendered, or been deprived of his all, and yet forced to labour under the hourly terrors of a gaol, in a wretched state of silent dependence upon a villain, the feelings of nature take a course, which nothing but the higher principles of religion, or a sense of honour, can obstruct—the former unhappily now possessing but little influence over even the lower ranks—the latter, in no respect adapted to their habits. He has proved, as he thinks, the folly of being honest;

and

and learns to defpife, or deteſt, thofe laws which, inſtead of protecting him, when he had done his utmoſt to difcharge the obligations he lay under, furnifh chains to bind him down to mifery without end.

Thus he is foon qualified to become the inſtrument and confederate of his former oppreffor.

The general obloquy of the public has long ſtigmatized a fet of men who bring difcredit upon a very ufeful branch of the profeffion of the law, and many worthy individuals who belong to it, by thofe enormous and inconceivable iniquities which they daily and hourly commit, among the ignorant, the needy, the diftreffed, and unprotected. They ply in all the haunts of vice, or of vulgar diffipation. They help forward the wicked, and liften to the tale of the fimple. They catch at every difhoneſt wifh; mount it into a claim; and are intruſted with the invention of means, and conduct of meafures, to perfect it into the legal form of a right—How is it that fuch wretches fubfift?—Upon the fruit of falfe arreſts; fictitious writs; determined perjuries; and bafe confpiracies!

The inferior officers of the law, from the bailiff to the follower's follower, are as keenly induſtrious as the lower order of attornies. But the laws, it is faid, have been provident in impofing fufficient checks and reſtraints upon their conduct.—Suppofing this to be true, is a poor ignorant creature, trembling under the horrors of a fudden arreſt, and deprecating the power of a mercenary and unprincipled tyrant, to appeal to the ſtatute book in the

moment

moment of diſtreſs; or look for evidence to the walls of a ſpunging-houſe?

It would be well if ſuch laws were inſtruments in the hands only of men who are poſſeſſed of that generous liberality of character which too frequently indeed ſuffers villainy to eſcape the laſh it deſerves, but feels no intereſt in the perſonal diſtreſs of an unfortunate debtor. The majority of creditors, in the circles of trade in particular, are of that deſcription. But there are many whoſe gains are dependent upon their power of oppreſſion.

Extortion is the ſafeſt of all the forms of robbery. It is generally practiſed under circumſtances which impoſe ſilence upon the ſufferer; and thoſe circumſtances the laws of impriſonment render perpetual. A poor friendleſs debtor is as much in durance, under the power of threats, as under the force of bolts. He is, for ever, at the diſpoſal of his creditor, and of courſe under his command.

If, then, the laws of impriſonment afford numberleſs temptations to fraud; are the means of extortion; and give ſubſiſtence to wretches who proſtitute the forms of law to the purpoſes of both, it will be difficult to defend them. Let ſuch offences, it may be ſaid, draw down upon the offenders all the rigour of exemplary puniſhment—Moſt certainly they ought to do ſo—But it is unneceſſary to prove *how much better it is for the legiſlature to withdraw temptations, than to preſcribe puniſhments.*

C H A P.

CHAP. XVII.

Reasons of Policy against the present Law of Imprisonment for Debt, founded upon its known Inefficacy, as a general Remedy, to the fair and honest Creditor.

THE certain expence of the proceeding; the severity of the measure; its well-known general inefficacy, as a remedy to the honest creditor*; and the trouble it may occasion; are strong circumstances, which must weigh in the mind of every rational man, in common prudence, against the imprisonment of his debtor. That measure, therefore, would seldom be adopted, if these circumstances were not overbalanced by other considerations. Yet there is but one single consideration which the law can recognize, as a just object of the creditor's proceedings; namely, *the prevention of fraud in the debtor*; or, in other words, *the enforcement of such a satisfaction as it may be in his power to give.*

But if that were to be held as the only purpose in the mind of a creditor which the present law of civil imprisonment endured, there would be an end of the subject of these reflections. In that case no.

---

* Were it not perfectly well known, and universally acknowledged, that the fair creditor is very rarely indeed the richer, but very frequently the reverse, by imprisoning his debtor, it might be proper here to be particular in stating circumstances to warrant a general conclusion on this subject.

hasty,

hasty, unprincipled exercise of the power of imprisonment; no unjust attempts to practise on the benevolence of others; no possibility of perpetual confinement (but as the punishment of some specific crime) would be suffered. An inquiry into something more than the bare existence of a debt would precede so strong an exertion of authority at the suit of a private party: a proceeding somewhat more solemn than the mere issuing of a writ of course, would be required to confirm, as just and necessary, a total forfeiture of a debtor's personal liberty.

The prevention of fraud, or the just enforcement of a satisfaction in the power of the debtor, cannot then, it is manifest, form the only object, in the view of a creditor, to which the law of imprisonment gives its aid. It gives the same aid, of course, to malice, to resentment, or the most corrupt and profligate purpose which can be supposed ever to actuate a man who stands in the legal character of a creditor. And these, it has been shewn, are likely to be at least very frequent inducements to a measure, which is, in itself, so generally unprofitable.

But is it fit that those municipal laws, from which manners must gradually receive their current and direction, should give countenance and support to such principles of conduct? In vain shall it be said that the laws cannot possibly distinguish between the honest pursuit of a just satisfaction, and such iniquitous purposes.—They cannot indeed distinguish if they do not inquire.

CHAP.

CHAP. XVIII.

The Law of Imprisonment for Debt considered with a View to the present State of those Frauds which it was meant to restrain.

IF the law of imprisonment for debt, in its full extent, had, to balance its manifold faults and infirmities, the merit of any efficacy in (what it chiefly professes) the suppression of fraud and extravagance, there would, comparatively speaking, exist but little of these vices in this country.

Is this then the fact? The question need hardly be answered. In the metropolis of England alone there is perhaps a more wonderful variety of fraudulent arts, than in all the world besides. Banditti of various forms, in the garb of every rank, and with the privileges of every profession, infest it in all quarters, from its purlieus to the court. Every species of lure is displayed for the deception of the wife, as well as of the unwary. New and unheard-of devices are brought daily into practice; and new words must be added to the language, in order to describe the practitioners. Some are trading, or mercantile adventurers; who for a course of years have been shewing false colours to the world; have put their signatures to a thousand lyes; planted partnerships in every quarter of the kingdom, to afford *names* for the circulation of fictitious credit; and, with

with all the port and appendages of wealth, have been conscious that in truth their capitals were insufficient to purchase the paper on which their falsehoods were written. To such men—even to such men—the certificate of bankrupt, too frequently affords its protection. Some are less eminent adventurers. They have no home; they are for ever on the wing; they vary both scene and character as circumstances suggest, and elude inquiry and detection with all the slight of long habit and practice. Others are more open and exposed—but these are cool determined villains, who think lightly of a gaol, and even rely for protection upon their abandoned characters. Nor are they disappointed. *They* have no friends: *they* possess no man's regard; therefore none will satisfy a creditor for their relief.

This is the present state of *fraud:* and as to extravagance, the folly which leads to fraud, seldom fails to shew itself in every species of wanton expence and dissipation. There is a dignity of mind about a man of integrity, which cannot relish the enjoyments of a desperate and unprincipled profusion. They certainly never amount to happiness—for villainy has always at least enough of reflection to make itself miserable.

But are not these banditti, it may be asked, liable to be interrupted by the laws of imprisonment as insolvent debtors? They are; but only in common with those who become innocently insolvent through misfortune, and with many chances of escaping which honest men have not. A creditor who first acted from passion, may afterwards act

from

ON CIVIL IMPRISONMENT.

from prudence. In time his anger cools; and the same intereſt which determines him to prolong his honeſt debtor's confinement, in expectation that the unfortunate man's worth may induce ſome friend to pity and relieve him, will alſo determine him to turn looſe upon the world thoſe abandoned wretches, who have grofsly defrauded him, and for whom no man will interfere. All this *they* know and anticipate; and having alſo, in common with honeſt debtors, the chance of certain laws, under the ſhelter of which they can eſcape in the croud, they conſider impriſonment for debt as a ſlight and familiar occurrence; never in their eyes diſgraceful, and often deſirable.

CHAP. XIX.

The remarkable Provision contained in the Statute commonly called the LORDS ACT.

WE are not left at liberty by a favourable presumption, founded upon the supposed impossibility of making distinctions, to vindicate the laws of civil imprisonment, when they act as instruments of private oppression. There is no room for presumption. The voice of the legislature has, by repeated acts, solemnly declared, that every man has a right, *at a certain expence*, to gratify himself by the imprisonment of his insolvent debtor.

By the 32 Geo. II. c. 28, commonly called *The Lords Act*, which was founded upon the 2 Geo. II. c. 22, and five subsequent amending or reviving acts *, and was confirmed and extended (only four years ago) by 26 Geo. III. c. 44, a variety of regulations are provided, for the purpose, among others, of compelling such insolvent debtors as shall be imprisoned for no greater sum, each, than £.200 †, to do all in their power for the satisfaction of their creditors, by surrendering every thing in the world that belongs to them—nay, more—by pledging (and it is just they should do so) their future industry,

---

* The 2 Geo. II. c. 22, was altered by 3 Geo. II. c. 27; explained and amended by 8 Geo. II. c. 24; continued by 14 Geo. II. c. 34, and 21 Geo. II. c. 33; and revived by 29 Geo. II. c. 28; which being allowed to expire, the 32 Geo. II. c. 28 was immediately enacted.—See Burr. Reports, 799.

† By the 32 Geo. II. c. 28, the sum was £.100.

the

ON CIVIL IMPRISONMENT. 109

the fruits of their labour, for the full payment of their former debts.

To a man of plain underftanding, with common notions of juftice, it would feem that here the law had amply done its office. But this ftatute—an Act of Grace—fays, No: the legiflature muft preferve inviolate the right of the creditor to what ftill remains, namely, *to the body of his debtor*. They may *invite* him to part with it: they may burden the exercife of his right with the expence of preferving the exiftence of that which is the fubject of it: they may clog the gratification of his paffions and refentments with terms which may tempt him to forego the fatisfaction: but they muft fecure it to him as it may be his pleafure to enjoy it.

And fo it is ordered. After the ftatute has fatiffied every particle of fubftantial intereft, immediate or contingent, which the creditor can have in the poor prifoner's confinement (in expectation, doubtlefs, that, for the good of the public, his perfon fhall then be reftored to the community) it is formally and folemnly, by a fpecial claufe for that purpofe, put in the power of the creditor, without affigning a reafon, to ftep in between the public and his debtor; ftill to infift upon the confinement of the poor prifoner's body, for the fatisfaction of his own malice and caprice, or the accomplifhment of fome fecret and unjuftifiable purpofe.

Thus a public law, enacted for public purpofes, is at once to be defeated, by a fpiteful, difhoneft, or defigning individual!

But

But this legal transgression against every principle of policy and sentiment of sound humanity, is not to be committed by an individual without expence. The creditor must pay *four pence a day* for the purpose of keeping the body of his debtor alive. The sullen pride of a low tyrant is gratified by the price: it makes the prisoner still more his own: he throws down his groat; and while he has a daily groat to give, his wretched debtor's imprisonment is prolonged, and may continue, during the tedious course of a vile existence *.

* Those who are not professional men will here be apt to suspect that the author has misstated the import of this extraordinary, modern, law; as in truth it is in general but little adverted to. An extract from the statute shall therefore be given. It enacts (section 13) That all prisoners who have made a fair assignment and conveyance of their estates and effects, and submitted to repeated examinations, in the manner prescribed by the act, shall be discharged, " *unless* such " creditor or creditors who shall have charged any such prisoner " or prisoners in execution as aforesaid, his, her, or their ex- " ecutors or administrators, *doth or do insist upon such prisoner* " *or prisoners*" (who had before fairly discovered and given up every thing) " *being detained in prison*; and shall agree by writ- " ing, signed with his, her, or their name or names, mark or " marks, or under the hand of his, her, or their attorney, in " case any such creditor or creditors, &c. shall be out of Eng- " land, *to pay and allow weekly such a sum, not exceeding two* " *shillings and four pence, as any such court shall think fit, unto the* " *said prisoner, to be paid every Monday in every week*, so long as " any such prisoner shall continue in prison in execution at the " suit of any such creditor or creditors: *and in every such case* " *every such prisoner and prisoners*" (after having done every thing possible for the satisfaction of creditors) " *shall be re-* " *manded back to the prison or gaol from whence he, she, or they* " *was or were so brought up, there to continue in execution.*"—The

reader

ON CIVIL IMPRISONMENT.

reader shall look in vain, throughout all the different provisions in this act, for any possible means by which such honest and unfortunate prisoners can be rescued from perpetual imprisonment. If their weekly pittances are regularly paid they are completely forlorn.

To torture the compassion of friends (as *Lord Mansfield* emphatically expresses it) and by that means extort payment from those who are not bound for the debt, is probably the general object of so gross a proceeding. But it may arise from various motives. Many a gallant veteran, whose knowledge of affairs hardly ever extended beyond the lines of a camp, or the limits of that little characteristical world which a ship of war contains, duped into insolvency, and irritated by wrongs, has by rough unpolished manners provoked the anger of his creditor, and been thus wretchedly fed in gaol for his imprudence. There are men even of integrity, who can in such a case forgive the injury, but not the insult; and convert the laws of their country into instruments of resentment. Many other instances might be supposed; and one other shall be mentioned. All the generous sensibilities of manhood revolt at the idea, but it is certain that the cold depravity of vice may suggest a motive for thus loading with misery a solitary and unprotected woman.—See Appendix H H.

CHAP.

CHAP. XX.

An Argument founded upon the frequent Inſtitution of CHARITABLE SOCIETIES *for the Relief of inſolvent Debtors in Priſon.*

THE heart of man is, doubtleſs, improved by knowledge. This is an enlightened, and a charitable age; and if there is much vice, there is alſo much virtue in the world.

In an age of refinement, when compared with ſimpler times, the modes of vice are more various, and (much it is to be lamented) they are thereby more generally diffuſed among the people. But the modes of virtue are alſo more ſocial, rational, and humane. The virtue of a Barbarian is debaſed by that pride which accompanies ignorance: while the virtue of a cultivated character can regulate or direct the ſenſibilities of nature, for the good of others; and tranſmit, unſeen, its generous and beneficent influence to thoſe who know not the hand that helps them.

In ſuch an age the general ſenſe of the people demands the reſpect of the legiſlature. There muſt be ſomething wrong when the deliberate, collected, charity of humane aſſociations, is ſeen making efforts (too often in vain) to raiſe up, not a fallen individual, but *a whole body of men*, whom the law has

thrown

ON CIVIL IMPRISONMENT.

thrown down. There are errors and infirmities, which enter into the motive, where the object is an individual, suffering under the eye of the benevolent. In such instances, the mind is generally too much occupied by compassion for the sufferer, to think of the cause for which he suffers. But it is not so when the attention is directed to the idea of a whole body of men, in the aggregate, placed in a deplorable situation by the law. There, the nature of the cause is the first object of reflection. A robber, or a thief, in chains, and under sentence of death, meets with compassion; and, for the moment, his offence is forgotten: but no such feeling arises, to lead off the judgment from the nature of the thing, when the idea of such offenders, *in general*, and the situation, to which, as such, they are reduced, is presented to the mind. The *feelings* of men are affected by the circumstances of individuals; but it is their *reason* which chiefly acts upon the collective situation of a whole body.

The melancholy case of many prisoners for debt has become matter of much concern to those who can reason as well as feel. Subscriptions are set on foot—societies are established*—representations are published, and the people are solicited to assist their unhappy fellow-creatures who labour under a species of distress, which no length of time can alleviate, or effort of the sufferers remove.

It has already been said—it has often been said, and it cannot be too often repeated, *that neither in the civil nor the criminal code, ought laws ever to*

* Appendix II.

wound the general sense of the people: and if, in any case, that general sense can be collected, it certainly may, respecting the laws of civil imprisonment. They confound the plain distinctions of reason, between right and wrong; they shock the understandings of mankind, by exhibiting precisely in the same situation, two characters notoriously the reverse of each other. They tend, in consequence, to destroy that reciprocal confidence between the governor and the governed, which, in a free country, is the principle of obedience; and they transfer the general prejudice, which ought always to affect those against whom such laws are executed, to those who execute them.

CHAP.

CHAP. XXI.

Acts of Insolvency.

THE general nature of these acts is well-known. They have already been mentioned; but the subject demands that they should be particularly examined. They have been applied as public remedies; but if they assume a beneficial appearance, by suppressing, for a time, some of the symptoms, while in fact they add virulence to the disease, it is time that the delusion should give way to something more substantially and permanently remedial.

An act of insolvency is defined to be " An occa-
" sional act, frequently passed by the legislature,
" whereby *all persons whatsoever*, who are either in
" too low a way of dealing to become bankrupts,
" or, not being in a mercantile state of life, are not
" included within the laws of bankruptcy, are dis-
" charged from all suits and imprisonment, upon
" delivering up all their estate and effects to their
" creditors, upon oath, at the sessions or assizes *."

By an act of insolvency then, all the members of the state declare their concurrence with the general

* 2 Blackst. Com. 484.

sense of the people, against the existing laws of civil imprisonment.

But by an act of insolvency the legislature takes abruptly from a creditor the privilege it had deliberately given him; and that too at the very moment when he is exercising it under the law as it stands, and to which he may fairly have trusted. Yet the same legislature refuses to prevent others from being so disappointed in future by a similar interruption—that is, they will not prohibit, restrain, or regulate the exercise of the privilege by any *prospective* law; but after suffering creditors *bonâ fide* to act, they will then on a sudden, and by *retrospect*, counteract them.

An act of insolvency, if it has any principle at all, must proceed upon the principle of its being either an act of mercy, or an act of justice, or an act of policy.

An act of *mercy*, that is, a public pardon for a public crime, it cannot be; because the prisoners relieved have never been tried and found guilty of any crime. Their imprisonment was inflicted by private hands, and (except in exigencies of state) neither punishment nor pardon can be directed to any *body of men* without discrimination; both must have an individual for their object, and special circumstances for their cause.

As an act of *justice*, it cannot with any consistency be considered:—for then the imprisonment and detention of debtors were acts of injustice; and the legislature would be accusing themselves of having

failed

ON CIVIL IMPRISONMENT.

failed in the essential duty of protecting the people from a long continued course of oppression, practised in their sight, at the same time that they refused to take any measures for preventing such acts of oppression in time to come.

And as an act of *policy*, it can with as little consistency be considered: for if there was any policy or utility in suffering so many individuals to be locked up from society, for an unlimited time, and without the means of relief, there can be none in bringing them back with blunted feelings, corrupted manners, and blasted characters.

Acts of insolvency impose no other terms upon insolvent debtors than those which every honest insolvent debtor imposes upon himself. But dishonest debtors, who must be compelled to do what is just, have the same measure served out to them; *they* also are relieved; because those acts make no distinction, and proceed upon no such inquiries as can exclude the unworthy. They operate in favour of " *all* " *persons whatsoever.*"—The rumour of an intended act of insolvency fills the gaols with all the unprincipled banditti who can get confederates to arrest them for the occasion*.

It is little the part of the legislature to strike blindly, from the impulse of the moment, at the regular effect of what it still holds to be law. Let laws be corrected wherever they are inconsistent or unjust;

---

* The act, it will be said, provides several preventives of this.—But is it in fact, or can it in the nature of things, be prevented?

but let the people be taught that, while the laws remain, no power can, by retrospect, controul the free course of their execution.

The laws of civil imprisonment strike promiscuously at all, least they should miss the guilty; and acts of insolvency operate indiscriminately in favour of all, least they should miss the innocent.

CHAP. XXII.

Recapitulation.

IT is now time to look back, and recal to mind the substance of what has been said.

THAT which determines the judgment to view with veneration and respect, whatever in law, or in legal practice, has been long established, is the just and fair presumption, that it was originally established by the wisdom of our ancestors for the good of the people. Destroy that presumption, and there is an end of its consequence. The laws of imprisonment have, therefore, been traced from their origin. It has been shewn that at first their operation was extremely limited, both with respect to persons and to things; that the arts of dishonest practice were the means by which they were carried far beyond both the common law and the acts of the legislature; that they grew into use, and assumed the character of legal procedure, by the deceptions of gross falsehood and pitiful verbal evasion; that they were extended by the parliament of Henry the seventh, under the administration of *Empson* and *Dudley* *, without re-

---

* These two profligate lawyers, who have been already mentioned, tainted the very source of justice and good government— One of them was speaker of the house of commons—*and they were both hanged.*

straint, diſtinction, or limitation, to almoſt all ſorts of civil tranſaction; that the miſeries and miſchiefs which were the neceſſary conſequence of theſe ſolemn deviations from juſtice, were upwards of a century ago deſcribed in an inſtrument which proves every word which it ſtates, namely, the ſtatute of Charles the ſecond, for the prevention of vexatious arreſts; and that many of the worſt evils which are there deſcribed are ſtill exiſting.

The *immediate* effects of the laws of civil impriſonment have been examined; and they have preſented one ſcene of miſery, inequality, and inconſiſtency.

Their *conſequential* effects have alſo been examined: they have been found to give colour and legal form to fraud; encouragement to the worſt propenſities in nature; the means of oppreſſion to the unjuſt; and an illuſory ſatisfaction to the injured.

The attempt has been made to try their wiſdom by their principle—but, conſidering them in their full extent, no regular principle has been diſcovered.

The experiment has further been made, by reaſoning upon their policy, in reſpect to the intereſts
of

of trade. But if they have there any influence at all, it is to give wings to *fictitious credit*; and facility to the course of extravagance.

Finally, those means of relief which, with a timid and irresolute hand, are held forth by the law to the wretched prisoner who happens to be confined for debts within a certain amount, on condition that it shall please his creditor to suffer such means of relief to have effect; and that occasional interposition of the legislature, by act of insolvency, which, with a retrospect, disappoints the execution it approves, have, upon examination, been found to carry along with them all the weakness, inconsistency, and danger of little expedients.

CHAP.

CHAP. XXIII.

CONCLUSION—*containing the Principles and general Lines of a Plan for amending the Laws of Civil Imprisonment.*

IT must be apparent to all who observe the proceedings of the superior courts of law, that their practice is now distinguished by a steady regard for the personal liberty of the subject. They are strict in its vindication, and liberal in whatever may tend to advance it. But the liberality of courts must be *correct*. Their rules and orders are to be bounded by those fixed and positive lines, which give stability to their determinations, and certainty to the laws they administer. The evils which have been described go far beyond their power. The legislature must therefore interpose; and it is full time that they should. For it concerns the honour as well as the immediate happiness of the country, that so foul a stain should be wiped from the system of our municipal law, as the possibility of inflicting perpetual imprisonment upon an unfortunate debtor; while fraud and iniquity, in their most palpable forms, are suffered to pass with impunity—And it will not be found that the difficulty in attaining the object is proportioned to its importance.

In proposing any material alteration upon a whole system of law, the following general propositions ought never to escape our recollection.

That

That theoretical or speculative ideas of perfection (which exists but in the imagination) have a tendency rather to obstruct than to promote the attainment of real and permanent improvement.

That the best system which can, with most simplicity, be reduced into practice, and not the best which can abstractly be conceived, is therefore the substantial object of our pursuit.

That zeal for the prevention of certain evils is often blind to the danger of admitting others, of a different nature, but equally or more pernicious in their consequences.

And that in amending or altering established laws, the legislature ought ever to be more guarded and circumspect than in the original formation of laws for new cases: because the spirit of reformation is often rash and intemperate; and though seldom dishonest, is always partial.

With these general ideas in view, the principles of a law to be proposed, for the purpose of bringing civil imprisonment to act with consistency and effect, may be suggested and considered with sufficient caution.

The subject in general naturally divides itself into two parts.

The *first* respecting those laws which relate to the arrest and imprisonment of *defendants*, upon what is called *mesne* process, in actions.

The *second*, respecting the imprisonment of *debtors in execution*.

But

But to avoid repetition, the principles and ideas which are to form the subject of the present Chapter shall be ranged under the following Sections.

SECT. I.

Of the Arrest of Defendants.

THERE are many cases in which the plaintiff's power of sudden arrest is just and necessary: and it ought to be a first principle, that in such cases the power of immediate arrest should be within the reach of *every* plaintiff without distinction. It would ill become the impartiality of the law to abridge the poor man's remedy, by throwing obstructions in his way which he could not possibly remove. Therefore, whatever provision may be made in directing the subsequent proceedings, with a view to possible cases, no preliminary security ought to be required of a plaintiff before the arrest; because that poverty which possibly arose from the very injury of which he complained, might deprive him of the means of satisfaction or redress.

On the other hand, no arrest of the defendant ought to take place unless where the plaintiff can make oath to *circumstances*, within certain lines of description, which may be drawn by the law*: for the simple assertion (though upon oath) of one man that another owes him a certain sum of money, can never in reason be deemed, of itself, sufficient.

---

* Let it be remembered, that this applies only to the arrest of *defendants*—no restriction is to be proposed of the arrest of *debtors* in execution, which requires no affidavit.

The

The affidavit ought to state, in addition to the debt, either that the defendant obtained the credit by artifice and deception — *Or*, as the plaintiff has reason to believe, that he intends to conceal himself or abscond in order to avoid his creditors — *Or* that he has fraudulently secreted or conveyed away, or is about fraudulently to secrete or convey away, his estate or effects — The circumstances upon which the plaintiff's belief is founded, to be positively stated. This affidavit, when allowed and indorsed by a judge as sufficient, ought to entitle the plaintiff to his writ or bill for immediately arresting the defendant.

The general purpose of an arrest is to procure bail; which is an additional security obtained by the interposition of judicial authority. But an additional security cannot in justice be demanded of a mere defendant, when there are not special circumstances to warrant that extraordinary interposition. As therefore, on the one hand, there are few cases where the defendant truly ought to be arrested on the commencement of the action, or during the subsequent proceedings, in which the plaintiff could not safely make oath in such terms as have been suggested; so, on the other, the alteration proposed would of course prevent a number of imprisonments which take place under the present law, in cases where the defendant ought never to have been arrested.

To diminish the number of arrests upon actions would, doubtless, be beneficial to the public. The defendant, when arrested, must either give bail to the sheriff or go to prison; and it will be found that by far the greater number of arrests take place,

place, either where an arrest is unnecessary, the defendant being sufficiently able to answer the event; or fruitless, the defendant not being able to find bail or satisfy the debt; or where the bail are duped and imposed on by the defendant, and the debt in the end only changes hands—For the alternative of a gaol is a strong temptation to dishonesty. A defendant who has been merely unfortunate, and, of course, innocently insolvent as respecting the plaintiff, may be thus tempted to act dishonestly towards his bail, in deluding them by a false account of his situation and affairs. The plaintiff recovers his money of the bail, and the bail become plaintiffs. The debt is still due by the defendant; and the law has only had the effect to satisfy one man at the expence of others, and to induce a fraud which would not have been committed if the defendant had not been arrested.

When to such instances are added the numberless examples of arrest for the purposes of extortion or oppression, there is surely weight enough in the scale to counterbalance the advantages which may, in some very rare and special cases, be derived from the arrest of defendants under the present law, where the plaintiffs could not have made oath to *any* of the circumstances stated in the affidavit proposed.

In judging of several original expedients for new cases, that which has upon the whole the balance in point of utility or advantage in its favour, though that balance should be but inconsiderable, is to be preferred. But in judging of a proposed alteration
of

ON CIVIL IMPRISONMENT.

of law, the benefits to be derived from the alteration must be comparatively great before an established law should be shaken. Deciding therefore by the latter rule, with every possible degree of caution, the restraint suggested upon the arrest of defendants would seem to be expedient.

SECT. II.

The Case of Defendants imprisoned at the Suit of Men who have neither Substance nor Character.

IT is certain that there are many evils arising from the mere abuse of the law, which it is impossible to prevent. But that idea has too often the effect of dissuading from every attempt to discourage such abuses, and thereby, in part, to prevent them. It is the subject of daily complaint, that actions are brought, and obstinate litigations maintained by designing or adventurous men, either in their own names, or in the names of others, who, though persons existing, have little or no interest in the event. It happens, therefore, too often, that when a defendant has at length, after a vexatious litigation, obtained a verdict, he has not the most distant chance of ever recovering his costs. Yet he must pay his attorney, and may of course be ruined.

Such hardships it is impossible in the common course of practice entirely to prevent, without striking too strongly at the civil rights of every individual.

But when a defendant has been arrested, and must lie

lie in prison during the whole course of such a cause; if not relieved by the law, there might in certain circumstances be means devised for his release upon proper cause shewn; even although the affidavit should be complete, and nothing relevant against the arrest could be stated.

In certain particular cases, for reasons peculiar to the nature of the actions, a rule may be obtained to stay proceedings till a *responsible* plaintiff is named. And wherever the plaintiff resides beyond the reach of the law of England, a similar rule may be obtained to stay proceedings till he give security for the costs *. Although therefore a plaintiff ought not to be obstructed in arresting the defendant wherever he can make oath to certain circumstances, yet the above cases afford precedent for the introduction of a rule by which a defendant might obtain his discharge from prison, unless the plaintiff gave security for costs, and eventual damages on account of the imprisonment, if it appeared upon trying the matter, on affidavits to circumstances, that the plaintiff was not a *responsible* person, *and* that the defendant ought to be so discharged: for it might appear from circumstances, that although the plaintiff was not, in point of substance, a responsible person, or could not give security, yet the defendant ought not to be discharged out of custody. A line might be drawn for that purpose, without limiting the court to precise descriptions, and yet without giving that loose discretionary power, the exercise of which is as difficult and oppressive to an upright judge, as it is dangerous to the public.

* Appendix K K.

SECT.

SECT. III.

The Case of a Defendant who has been arrested and kept in Prison during the whole Course of the Proceedings; and yet finally obtains a Judgment in his Favour.

IT is hardly possible to conceive a case, against the hardship and injustice of which the understanding more forcibly revolts, than that of a defendant, who, to the ruin of himself and his family, has lain in prison for a tract of time at the suit of a plaintiff who has proceeded perhaps by way of experiment, and is eventually found to have had no foundation whatever for his action—and yet this injured man has no means of satisfaction: for costs are no more than a reimbursement; and not even so much. An action for damages lies where the arrest can be shewn to have been malicious, or such as the plaintiff himself certainly knew to be clearly groundless: but innumerable instances occur of arrests which are groundless and vexatious, but where a defendant who has lain for months in gaol has no redress whatever.

If, however, it is impossible to devise any means for removing, in a considerable degree, the hardship above described, which defendants, who have been so imprisoned, must frequently suffer under the present law, without putting plaintiffs in a situation of too much danger, the evil must be classed with those to which, in the imperfect state of all human institutions, the people must submit. For as, in the formation of rules for regulating the course of judicial proceedings, it is a leading principle that the avenues to justice are to be preserved as free and open as possible, that principle could have little effective utility if suitors were discouraged, by the apprehension of eventual damages, from the prosecution of claims which appeared to be just, or the use of measures which circumstances suggested as prudent or necessary.

But there is surely no such impossibility. As in the case of malicious or grossly vexatious arrests, where the law, as already observed, has given an action, an action might be given in ordinary cases; and the powers of the jury, under the direction of the judge, in case of verdict for the defendant, or of the judge by *certificate* (no novelty in the law), in case of nonsuit, might be so extended as to remove the ground of complaint; which is not that *every* defendant who has been imprisoned, and yet obtains judgment in his favour, cannot have redress or reparation for the imprisonment he has suffered; but that there exist no possible means, if malice or vexatious purpose cannot be positively shewn, by which *any* defendant who has been so imprisoned upon a groundless action can receive such reparation. It would seem that the verdict or certificate proposed might be so applied by a very simple as well as safe and practical course of proceeding.

SECT. IV.

Imprisonment of DEBTORS *in Execution.*

THE present law of imprisonment of debtors in execution is of so little avail to creditors, that almost every alteration to be proposed on that branch of civil imprisonment must have for its immediate object the interest of the *creditor*. As the law now stands, the imprisoning creditor may only obtain an ideal satisfaction, and *must*, in consequence, suffer a substantial loss: for he must lose his right of execution against the substance of his debtor, that is, against his lands and goods, during his life.

It is therefore an idea too manifest to require the support of argument, that the creditor's right of execution against the lands or goods of his debtor, should remain unaffected by the imprisonment. For *imprisonment is only for the purpose of discovery; or of inducing the debtor to do all that he can for his creditor's satisfaction*; and ought never to be considered as in itself a satisfaction*.

Nor can it be said that thus the creditor might have a double remedy; or that while he imprisoned his debtor for the purpose of compelling him to discharge the debt, he might at the same moment deprive him of the means of discharging it, by seizing

* See part ii. chap. viii. *supra*.

his effects. The creditor might or might not seize the debtor's estate or effects, as he should think proper; but if he did, he would of course be obliged, by an express provision in the law for that purpose, to give notice when he levied or recovered his debt by such means; and the debtor's discharge out of custody at his suit would follow the satisfaction so obtained.

SECT. V.

The Discharge of Insolvent Debtors.

ON the one hand it can hardly be the subject of doubt, that the *possibility* of perpetual imprisonment for debt ought not to be endured by the law. On the other, the proper ends and purposes of imprisonment must not be defeated, but are on the contrary to be promoted.

If the law knew no such remedy as imprisonment for debt, and a creditor were confined to his execution against the estate or effects, the debtor might not only refuse payment of the debt, but withhold all means of satisfaction, by concealing, secreting, or covering his effects from the view of his creditors. This serves to point out the objects which the laws of imprisonment *ought* to profess—and it would seem that they may be reduced to the following:

First, to induce the debtor, if he has money, to apply it; and if he has not, to procure it, by means of his effects, for the purpose of discharging the debt.

debt. This is indeed the professed object of the present law.

Secondly, to compel him to *discover* his estate and effects, in order that the creditor himself may be able to take measures for his own satisfaction. This cannot be an object of the present law, because the creditor cannot avail himself of any such discovery, by proceeding against his imprisoned debtor's estate or effects.

Thirdly, to expose *extravagance* or *negligence* to public animadversion, and punishment.

And *lastly*, to subject the conduct and affairs of insolvent debtors to strict examination, for the purpose of relieving the honest, and bringing the *fraudulent* to public trial and conviction.

While such objects, or any of them, are attainable, imprisonment acts upon principles which are plain and intelligible. But a debtor who lies in gaol under circumstances which demonstrate that the further duration of his confinement cannot lead to any one of those objects, is deprived of his personal freedom against good policy as well as justice. As matter of common right, founded upon eternal and unalterable laws, he is therefore entitled to have it restored to him.

But the question is, how can such lines be drawn, or general rules established, by which it may be determined when imprisonment, in every particular case, has done its office, and when it ought to cease? The question is answered thus:

For a certain given time * the debtor's confine-

---

* Suppose *three months* from the commencement of the debtor's imprisonment in execution.

ment might be considered merely as a mode of coercion, for the purpose of compelling him to satisfy the creditor or creditors at whose suit he stands imprisoned—And such a limited time it would be reasonable to give, without subjecting the debtor to any thing beyond the mere imprisonment: for a man whose intentions are honest may sometimes be so situated that he must go to gaol; and yet within a short time he may be able to provide the means of satisfaction.

But a person who has remained a debtor in execution beyond that given time, ought to be obliged, for the sake of the public as well as of creditors, to disclose the state of his affairs, in order that his creditors may judge of his conduct, and take proper measures for their own satisfaction, or public justice. He ought, therefore, to be obliged, at the expiration of that time, to deliver to the gaoler, for general inspection, a full statement of his affairs, with an account of the causes of his insolvency. There would in this be a degree of danger or of punishment, to certain characters, which might induce them to make every possible exertion, for satisfying the creditors at whose suit they stood imprisoned, either before any such general discovery should become necessary, or (if they made no such discovery at the time prescribed by the law) before they could be exposed to those subsequent proceedings, which, if they remained in gaol, would unavoidably take place, and bring their fraudulent practices to light.

A debtor who had remained still longer in prison, ought to be considered as a proper object of public

ON CIVIL IMPRISONMENT.

attention; for it would then be fair to presume either that the creditor or creditors at whose suit he had been so long in confinement, prolonged his imprisonment without any rational object; or that his conduct had been such, either in point of negligence, extravagance, or fraud, as to call for punishment at the hands of the public. In both cases he ought to be discharged out of custody as a debtor in execution; but in the latter he ought, on conviction, to suffer the punishment he deserved.

Every debtor, therefore, who had continued a certain time,[*] as a prisoner in execution, ought to be brought up in *Westminster-hall*; or, if in custody beyond a certain distance from London, at the *assizes*; where such proceedings, of a safe but summary nature, might take place under the special provision of the law [†], as would enable the judge, upon examination of the insolvent, and hearing the charges against him (if any were made), to determine, either that his farther imprisonment could answer no good purpose, to the creditors or to the public; in which case he ought immediately to be discharged as an insolvent debtor, and set at liberty —Or, that sufficient cause had been shewn by creditors, why he should be still longer detained a prisoner in execution; in which case he ought to be

---

[*] Suppose *six months* from the commencement of his imprisonment in execution; that is, three months after delivering an account of his affairs, and of the causes of his insolvency.

[†] As the present is only a *general* view of the plan proposed, the particular forms and proceedings here alluded to are not stated.

remanded

remanded as such—Or, that his insolvency had arisen from a gross degree of extravagance or negligence; in which case, though discharged as an insolvent debtor, he ought to be committed to prison for a limited time as a direct punishment—Or, that there were circumstances which fixed upon him suspicions of fraud sufficiently strong to warrant his commitment, for the purpose of preventing his escape (during a certain time) from the prosecution and punishment which the law ought to provide for such fraudulent insolvents; in which case, though discharged as an insolvent debtor from a fruitless execution, he ought to be so committed for safe custody.

A debtor might be *remanded* in execution on account of difficulty or particular circumstances in his case; but every debtor so remanded ought (if not discharged by his creditors) to be brought up a second time, either at Westminster-hall within a certain time, or at the next assizes, as the case might be: and, in order that imprisonment in execution might in all cases whatever have a limited duration, he ought then to be discharged as an insolvent debtor; but might be committed for punishment or trial, as the judge should see cause.

In this manner every debtor in execution would be discharged by the public, *out of that kind of custody*, at a certain period; and, if honest, he would have nothing to fear: but if he deserved punishment, he would stand justly exposed to it. Creditors would have all the advantages of imprisonment in

execution

execution which they can fairly enjoy at present; because their debtors would be in their power for a sufficient length of time to answer every just purpose—And, not to mention the great benefit of a concurrent remedy by execution against the debtor's estate and effects during his imprisonment, as well as after it, they would have this additional advantage, that dishonest debtors would then have cause to dread a gaol. For as cruelty or unjust design could carry oppression but a certain length, so fraud or dishonesty could never hope, after a certain time, to effect an escape by the influence of address, or through the weakness of compassion. The severities of a gaol would form an *Ordeal* for distinguishing the innocent from the guilty; and creditors, in vindicating their own private rights, would be promoting the course of public justice.

SECT. VI.

Of the ESTATE AND EFFECTS *of Persons discharged as Insolvent Debtors.*

IF creditors were to be denied (as they are at present) the power of proceeding against the estates or effects of their imprisoned debtors, it would be impossible to propose any permanent law for discharging insolvents, without particularly providing for the surrender of their effects to their creditors at large, as the condition of their discharge. It is an idea which naturally suggests itself; but every scheme, of which it forms a part,

part, involves in it a ground of unanfwerable objection. All the various forms and proceedings which, in fuch cafes, are indifpenfably neceffary for regulating the transfer of the debtor's eftate to his creditors; the inveftiture of truftees; the adminiftration of thofe truftees; the diftribution of the refidue, after the fund has been worn down to half its original fize; and the effect of that diftribution upon the creditor's claims againft the future eftate of the debtor, form a complicated machinery, full of the means of abufe; and too great, in general beyond all proportion, for the value and extent of the object*.

But if creditors could proceed in the regular courfe of execution, not only againft the eftates and effects of their infolvent debtors, during their imprifonment, and when difcharged as fuch, but alfo againft their future acquifitions, unlefs protected by the *certificate of bankrupt*; and had befides the benefit of pofitive laws to deter their debtors from the frauds of concealment or voluntary mifapplication of the means of fatisfaction in their power (which ought to form an effential part of every plan of amendment) the mere difcharge of their *perfons*, after every rational purpofe of imprifonment had been anfwered, could never fubftantially affect the rights of creditors; or be the proper ground of any new fet of meafures, to throw the courfe of law out of its ordinary channel.

* The Lords' Act, occafional infolvent acts, and the unavoidable abufe of the bankrupt laws, when applied to trifling cafes for the fole benefit of the bankrupt, afford examples of what is here ftated.

SECT.

SECT. VII.

The Effect of the Discharge of a Debtor as an Insolvent Debtor.

THE discharge of an insolvent debtor ought only to protect his person; and as, in every instance, the law should lean in favour of the creditor, that protection ought to be so qualified, that the burden of shewing himself entitled to it should be thrown upon the debtor: nor ought it to affect the right of a creditor who had not received timely notice of the debtor's imprisonment previous to his discharge. Therefore it might justly be part of the law, that before a discharged insolvent debtor, arrested and imprisoned upon a debt prior to his discharge, could be discharged out of custody upon such arrest, he should be obliged to shew, either that the creditor had notice of the former imprisonment served upon him a certain time before the insolvent's discharge; or that due enquiry had been made respecting such creditor's residence, without effect: and this might be shewn by the affidavit of the person who served the notice, or made the enquiry. On the other hand, a debtor so arrested or imprisoned for a debt, prior to his discharge as an insolvent debtor, at the suit of a creditor who had such regular notice of the insolvent's former imprisonment, previous to his discharge, ought to have his action for such subsequent arrest and imprisonment, and recover damages on proving such notice.

With respect to the case of a *bankrupt trader* thus discharged as an insolvent; the complaints which have often justly been made, that certificates of bankrupt are obtained with too much ease, regard in general the material operation of such certificates in protecting the *future effects* of the bankrupt. But the law now proposed would afford no cover to the future effects of an insolvent debtor; and therefore a bankrupt trader so discharged would in that essential respect be as much dependent upon the certificate as ever. His person indeed, though he were uncertificated, would be free from arrest for former debts—but that freedom could only be obtained after a previous imprisonment and proceedings which would aid and promote the operation of the bankrupt laws; and (in consequence of a provision in the law for that purpose) expose the bankrupt, as a discharged insolvent debtor, to eventual punishment, in certain cases, for which those laws do not provide.

SECT. VIII.

The Punishment of FRAUDS *committed by Persons who have been discharged as Insolvent Debtors.*

IT has been shewn to be one of the many bad consequences of imprisonment for debt, as now established, that as every insolvent debtor is liable to perpetual imprisonment, the frauds of insolvent debtors, considered merely as such, have never been the subject of precise legal description, and direct criminal prosecution. And yet there are many instances

instances of fraudulent conduct in insolvent debtors, which admit of precise description, and are too gross to escape the correction they deserve.

Besides the punishment, therefore, which might be inflicted for gross negligence or extravagance, by summary commitment, as already proposed, every person discharged as an insolvent debtor ought to be indictable for certain fraudulent acts, as correctly described in the law; any improper delay in delivering the statement of his affairs and causes of his insolvency required by the law, or in delivering an unfair statement, being of course so described as fraudulent. Upon conviction, every fraudulent insolvent debtor ought to be punishable by imprisonment, pillory, and transportation, singly or together, as the court, from circumstances, should think proper.

To be discharged as an insolvent debtor would, therefore, be no desirable object to those who might otherwise be disposed to avail themselves of that measure for dishonest purposes. To such persons it would be a measure full of danger.

SECT. IX.

Public Notice of the Proceedings respecting Insolvent Debtors.

WHATEVER may be the particular case of an individual who has unavoidably fallen by misfortune into a state of insolvency, it ought to be inculcated as a general idea, that a certain degree of of reproach is necessarily attached to that situation. It implies something wrong either in the principles, or the manners, or the prudence of the insolvent. It is a species of *prima facie* evidence against him.

It concerns the public, therefore, that persons who have been the subjects of legal proceedings as insolvent debtors should be known, as such, to the public. It does so for two reasons: *First*, because the reproach which necessarily belongs to the character, must induce men who have any regard for reputation to avoid a situation which exposes them so unfavourably to public observation: and, *Secondly*, because it is convenient that other men, in the most distant parts, should have an opportunity of knowing the fact, not only with a view to more than ordinary caution in future transactions with such persons; but in order that such discharged insolvents may be brought to trial and punishment, if they have been guilty of frauds described by the law, which may not have come to light in the course of the proceedings previous to their discharge.

But if this applies to the case of a mere insolvent, who may have been discharged as such without difficulty or hesitation, and immediately set at liberty, it must apply still more strongly, in different degrees, to the case of an insolvent who has been remanded as a debtor in execution, or committed either for palpable negligence or extravagance, or on suspicion of fraud.

It would, therefore, be no superfluous provision in a new law, to make it the duty of the proper officer

ficer of the court to publish without delay, in the London Gazette, a list of all insolvents brought up under the act, and either immediately discharged and set at liberty; or remanded as debtors in execution; or committed, immediately after their discharge as insolvents, for matters appearing against them.

THE Author now concludes—He has stated his ideas with that freedom which he feels to be consistent with infinite respect for the opinions of others, and a just impression of the magnitude and difficulty of the subject. It is not indeed for every individual to act the part of a legiflator; but every individual ought freely to state the suggestions of his mind upon those topics of common concern, which, from his situation and habits, have naturally engaged his attention: and he may be assured, that such suggestions will ever be best received by those who are best able to judge of them.

APPENDIX.

APPENDIX.

NOTE A, p. 6.

HABET rex etiam curiam et jufticiarios in banco refidentes qui cognofcunt de omnibus placitis de quibus auctoritatem habent cognofcendi; *et fine warranto jurifdictionem non habent nec coercionem.*—*Bracton, lib.* 3. *f.* 105.

NOTE B, p. 7.

Dicuntur brevia cum fint formata ad fimilitudinem regulæ juris quæ breviter et paucis verbis intentionem proferentis exponunt, ficut regula juris, rem quæ eft, breviter enarrat; non tamen ita debet effe breve, quin rationem et vim intentionis contineat.—*Fleta, lib.* 2; *c.* 12.

NOTE C, p. 7.

Thefe writs were of two different forts, and had two different technical appellations, viz. a *Præcipe*, and a *Si te fecerit fecurum:* the former, peculiar to certain actions where the defendant had an option given him either to do the thing required, or fhew caufe why he did not—the latter, peculiar to other actions, and commanding the defendant peremptorily, and in the first instance, to shew cause. But both required security or *pledges* from the prosecutor, as the condition of compelling the defendant to appear.

NOTE D, p. 9.

The course of those writs and proceedings was as follows:—A man was charged with the breach of an obligation purely civil; as for example, to pay a certain sum of money upon a day certain—the day of payment elapsed, and the creditor proceeded thus: He gave a short note of his claim into the office of Chancery; an original writ, or, as it is shortly termed, an *original*, was from thence issued; the creditor giving security either in Chancery, or afterwards before the sheriff, that he should prosecute the suit with effect. By virtue of the writ thus obtained from Chancery the debtor was commanded by the sheriff, in the king's name, either to pay the particular sum therein specified, or to appear upon a day certain before the king's justices at Westminster (the Court of *Common Pleas*) to shew cause why he did not. The jurisdiction of the court now attached upon the cause thus brought before it, by the writ from Chancery, and therefore it had authority to proceed afterwards by means of its own powers. The debtor disobeyed the writ from Chancery, and neither paid the money nor appeared in court. A writ then issued from the court itself, termed a writ of *pone* or *attachment* (which, with all subsequent writs, were called *judicial* writs, as proceeding from the court) directed also to the sheriff, by which he was commanded, in the king's name, to take certain of the debtor's goods which should be forfeited, and sureties who should be amerced (technically, *to take gage and safe pledges*) if he did not appear upon another day certain to answer to the demand, and to shew cause why he had

disobeyed

disobeyed the original writ. The debtor yet disobeyed—and still his person was free. Another writ issued, called a *distringas*, but it was only against his property. By it the sheriff was commanded to seize, in the king's name, all the debtor's lands and chattels within his county, and to answer for the issues and profits thereof, not to the creditor but to the king, who had a right to the whole forfeiture, in consequence of his subject's disobedience.—*Finch, l.* 352—3 *Blackst. Com.* 280.—A succession of these writs, one after another, might then issue *ad infinitum* (termed *distress infinite*) so as to deprive him from time to time of every thing he acquired, until he chose to obey the commands of his sovereign.

NOTE E, p. 10.

Where the injury was attended with violence, or was so charged, the original writ was joined with that which in the former case issued only in the second place, viz. the *pone* or *attachment*, by which the sheriff was ordered to take gage and pledges for the defendant's appearance; and yet another writ against his property, such as also issued in the former case, viz. the *distringas*, had to run its course. Nor was it till the sheriff had made a return *nihil* (as it is called) that is, given for answer to the writ, that the person charged had *nothing* within his county by the seizure of which he might be distressed, that a warrant was at length issued for bringing in his person to answer to the charge, which was termed a *capias ad respondendum*. Or if the sheriff of the county to whom the writ was directed (which was always the county where the court sate) returned for answer, that he could not find the defendant, then another writ, called a *testatum capias*, was issued, directed to the sheriff of another county, where it was said the defendant lurked; and repeated writs of the same sort

(called

(called *alius & pluries* writs) were succeffively iffued againft him. If not yet found, he was outlawed.

This was the regular courfe of proceeding; but according to the prefent practice the *capias*, or warrant to feize the defendant's perfon, is ufually the commencement of the action; a fictitious original writ and return being put upon record " to give a colour of regularity to the proceed-
" ings."

Thefe proceedings have been ftated upon the authority of Lord Coke, Lord Chief Baron Gilbert, Sir William Blackftone, and others—Nor is it material here to examine how far the authority of thefe great names in the law is fhaken by fome paffages in *Bracton*, with regard to the more ancient courfe of common law proceedings, fuppofed by fome to have taken place, in fuch perfonal actions. It appears certain, that at one period, at leaft, the proceedings eftablifhed by long practice were as they have been ftated—and, in many refpects, are the *regular* courfe of proceeding at this day.

NOTE F, p. 12.

This refers to the general fpirit of Magna Charta, and not to any article in particular. Chapter 29th of that great inftrument, indeed, is in the following words: " Nullus
" liber homo capiatur vel imprifonetur, aut diffeifietur de
" libero tehemento fuo, vel libertatibus, vel liberis confuetu-
" dinibus fuis, aut utlegatur, aut exuletur, aut aliquo modo
" diftruatur; nec fuper eum ibimus, nec fuper eum mitte-
" mus, nifi per legale judicium parium fuorum, *vel per legem*
" *terræ*." And upon this chapter an argument has been founded, to fhew that every fubfequent law, or practice recognized as law, which authorized imprifonment, except
upon

upon a trial by jury, is against Magna Charta. This argument is maintained in a book (which the author has perused since he wrote the preceding treatise) intituled, " *Considerations upon the Law of Insolvency,*" published by Mr. *Burgess* about eight years ago, in which much curious matter is collected, and a very full detail is given of all the statutes upon this subject. But the contrary opinion is held by many, who think with *Lord Coke*, that by the above article, qualified as it is by the words " *vel per* " *legem terræ*," it was meant " that no man" (unless by the verdict of a jury) " should be taken, imprisoned, or put " out of his freehold, without process of the law; that is, " by indictment or presentment of good and lawful men, " where such deeds be done, in due manner, *or by writ* " *original of the common law.*" 2 *Inst.* 50.——See also " *The History of the English Law,*" vol. ii. p. 442.

NOTE G, p. 14.

The writ which issued upon this statute against the bailiffs of lords, was called a writ of *monstravit de compoto*— See *Regiſtrum Brevium*, 136, F. N. B. 259. And the defendant's person was not only free, if he had any lands within the county, but he had in that case immediate relief and damages against the master he had defrauded, if, having lands, he was arrested by him upon the above writ, which necessarily averred that he had no lands within the county. For this purpose a special writ was given him, by which, without regard to his own fraud and offence, the loss of liberty only of a man who had lands in the county, was considered. The lord, his master, at whose suit he was imprisoned, is there said to have maliciously obtained the writ *de compoto* against him, " et sic eum, per corporis " sui attachiamentum multipliciter ea occasione gravari " procuravit,

" procuravit, in deceptione curiæ noſtræ, et grave dam-
" num ipſius, et contra legem et concilium regni noſtri
" Angliæ," &c.—The writ concluded with an order for
his releaſe.——*Regiſtrum*, 137—2 *Inſt*. 144.

This ſhews how heinouſly the ſpirit of the law felt itſelf, in thoſe days, offended by the impriſonment of a man, in the only civil caſe which could authorize his impriſonment, *if any other poſſible means occurred for enforcing the ſatisfaction demanded.*——And it was held (ſomewhat abſurdly indeed) that property, even to the ſmalleſt extent, afforded ſuch means.

NOTE H, p. 17.

The *ſtatute of merchants*, 13 Edw. I. ſt. 3 (anno 1285) is as follows: " Foraſmuch as merchants, which hereto-
" fore have lent their goods to divers perſons, be fallen in
" poverty, becauſe there is no ſpeedy remedy provided
" whereby they may ſhortly recover their debt at the day
" of payment; and for this cauſe many merchants do re-
" frain to come into the realm with their merchandize, to
" the damage of ſuch merchants, and of all the realm; the
" king and his council, at his parliament holden at *Acton*
" *Burnel,* after the feaſt of *St. Michael,* the eleventh year
" of his reign, ordained eſtabliſhments thereupon for the
" remedy of ſuch merchants; which ordinances and eſta-
" bliſhments the king commanded that they ſhall be firmly
" kept and obſerved throughout this realm, whereby mer-
" chants have had remedy, and have recovered their debts
" with leſs inconvenience and trouble than they have had
" heretofore. But foraſmuch as merchants after complained
" to the king, that ſheriffs miſinterpreted his ſtatutes,
" and ſometimes by malice and falſe interpretation delayed
" the execution of the ſtatute, to the great damage of mer-
" chants, the king, at his parliament holden at *Weſtminſter*
" after

" after *Easter*, the thirteenth year of his reign, caused the
" said statute made at *Acton Burnel* to be rehearsed; and for
" the declaration of certain articles in the statute aforesaid,
" hath *ordained* and *established*, that a merchant who will
" be sure of his debt shall cause his debtor to come before
" the *mayor of London*, or before some *chief warden* of a
" city, or of another good town where the king shall ap-
" point, and before the mayor and chief warden, or other
" sufficient men chosen and sworn thereto, when the mayor
" or chief warden cannot attend, and before one of the
" clerks that the king shall thereto assign, when both can-
" not attend, he shall acknowledge the debt, and the day of
" payment; and the recognizance shall be enrolled by one
" of the clerks hands being known, and the roll shall be
" double, whereof one part shall remain with the mayor,
" or chief warden, and the other with the clerks that
" thereto shall be first named; and further, one of the said
" clerks with his own hand shall write an obligation, to
" which writing the seal of the debtor shall be put with the
" king's seal provided for the same intent; which seal
" shall be of two pieces, whereof the greater piece shall
" remain in the custody of the mayor or the chief warden,
" and the other piece in the keeping of the foresaid clerk.
" And if the debtor do not pay at the day limited unto him,
" then shall the merchant come to the mayor or clerk with
" his obligation; and if it be found by the roll or writing
" that the debt was acknowledged, and the day of payment
" expired, the mayor or chief warden *shall cause the body of*
" *the debtor to be taken* (if he be Lay) whensoever he hap-
" peneth to come in their power, and shall commit him to
" the prison of the town, if there be any; and he shall remain
" there at his own costs until he hath agreed for the debt."
The original, *ex Rot. in Turr. Lond.* expresses this passage
thus: " *E si le dettur ne rende al jour qe lui est assis, si veigne*
" *le marchaunt al meyre e al clerk ove sa lettre de obligacion,*
" *e si trove seit par roule ou par lettre qe la ditte sust conue, e*
" *le*

" *le jour assis seit passe, si face le mayre ou chief gardeyn
" prendre le cors al dettur (sil est lay) quel heure qe il seit trove
" en son poer, et liverer a la prison de la vile, si prison y seite
" la demoerge a ses custages propres, desque ataunt qil eit
" set gre de la dette.*" " And it is commanded that the
" keeper of the town prison shall retain him upon the de-
" livery of the mayor or warden: and if the keeper shall
" not receive him he shall be answerable for the debt, if
" he have whereof; and if he have not whereof, he that
" committed the prison to his keeping shall answer. And
" if the debtor cannot be found in the power of the mayor
" or chief warden, then shall the mayor or chief warden
" send into the Chancery, under the king's seal, the recog-
" nizance of the debt; and the chancellor shall direct a writ
" unto the sheriff in whose shire the debtor shall be found,
" for to take his body (if he be Lay) and safely to keep
" him in prison until he hath agreed for the debt; and
" within a quarter of a year after that he is taken his
" chattels shall be delivered him, so that by his own he
" may levy and pay the debt; and it shall be lawful unto
" him, during the same quarter, to sell his lands and tene-
" ments for the discharge of his debts, and his sale shall
" be good and effectual. And if he do not agree within
" the quarter next after the quarter expired, all the lands
" and goods of the debtor shall be delivered unto the mer-
" chant by a reasonable extent, to hold them until such
" time as the debt is wholly levied, and nevertheless the
" body shall remain in prison as before is said; and the
" merchant shall find him bread and water." In the original it is thus expressed: " *E sil ne face gre dedenz le quar-
" ter passe seient liverez au marchaunt tutz les biens del deitter
" e totes ses terres, par resnable estent, a tenir desque ataunt qe
" la dette pleinement serra levee, e ja le plus tart le cors de-
" moerge en prison cum avaunt est dit, e le marchaunt luy
" truisse pain e ewe.*" " And the merchant shall have
" such seisin in the lands and tenements delivered unto him
" or his assignee, that he may maintain a writ of *novel*
" *desseisin,*

"*deſſeiſin*, if he be put out, and re-deſſeiſin alſo as of freehold,
" to hold to him and his aſſigns until the debt be paid; *and as
" ſoon as the debt is levied the body of the debtor ſhall be delivered
" with his lands.* And in ſuch writs as the chancellor doth
" award mention ſhall be made that the ſheriff ſhall certify
" the juſtices of the one bench or of the other, how he
" hath performed the king's commandment, at a certain
" day; at which day the merchant ſhall ſue before the
" juſtices, if agreement be not made; and if the ſheriffs do
" not return the writ, or do return that the writ came too
" late, or that he hath directed it to the bailiffs of ſome
" franchiſe, the juſtices ſhall do as it is contained in
" the latter ſtatute of *Weſtminſter*. And if in caſe the
" ſheriff return that the debtor cannot be found, or that
" he is a clerk, the merchant ſhall have writs to all the
" ſheriffs where he ſhall have land, and that they ſhall de-
" liver unto him all the goods and lands of the debtor by
" a reaſonable extent, to hold unto him and his aſſigns in
" the form aforeſaid; and at the laſt he ſhall have a writ to
" what ſheriff he will, to take his body (if he be Lay) and
" to retain it in manner foreſaid. And let the keeper
" of the priſon take heed that he muſt anſwer for the body,
" or for the debt. And after the debtor's lands be deliver-
" ed to the merchant, the debtor may lawfully ſell his land,
" ſo that the merchant have no damage of the approve-
" ments; and the merchants ſhall always be allowed for
" their damages, and all coſts, labours, ſuits, delays, and
" expences, reaſonable. And if the debtor find ſureties
" which do acknowledge themſelves to be principal debtors,
" after the day paſſed, the ſureties ſhall be ordered
" in all things as is ſaid of the principal debtor,
" as to the arreſt of body, delivery of lands, and other
" things. And when the lands of the debtors be delivered
" unto the merchant, he ſhall have ſeiſin of all the lands
" that were in the hand of the debtor, the day of the re-
" cognizance made, in whoſe hands ſoever that they come
" after, either by feoffment or otherwiſe. And after the

" debt

"debt paid, the debtor's lands, and the issues of lands of
"debtors by feofment, shall return again, as well to the
"feoffee as the other lands unto the debtors. And if the
"debtor or his sureties die, the merchant shall have no
"authority to take the body of his heir, but he shall have
"his lands, as before is said, if he be of age, or when he
"shall be of full age. And a seal shall be provided that
"shall serve for fairs, and the same shall be sent unto every
"fair under the king's seal by a clerk sworn, or by the
"keeper of the fair. And of the commonalty of the mer-
"chants of the city of London two merchants shall be
"chosen that shall swear, and the seal shall be opened be-
"fore them; and the one piece shall be delivered unto the
"foresaid merchants, and the other shall remain with the
"clerk; and before them, or one of the merchants (if both
"cannot attend) the recognizances shall be taken, as be-
"fore is said. And before that any recognizances be in-
"rolled, the pain of the statute shall be openly read be-
"fore the debtor, so that after he cannot say that any did
"put another penalty than that whereto he bound himself.
"And to maintain the costs of the said clerk, the king
"shall take of every pound a penny in every town where
"the seal is, except fairs, where he shall take one penny
"halfpenny of the pound. This ordinance and act the
"king willeth to be observed from henceforth throughout
"his realm of *England* and *Ireland*, amongst the which
"people they that will may make such recognizances (ex-
"cept *Jews*, to whom this ordinance shall not extend).
"And by this statute a writ of debt shall not be abated;
"and the chancellor, justices of the one bench and of the
"other, the barons of the exchequer, and justices errants,
"shall not be estopped to take recognizances of debts of
"those who are willing to acknowledge them before them:
"but the execution of recognizances made before them
"shall not be done in the form aforesaid, but by the law
"and manner before used, and otherwise provided in other
"statutes."

† The

APPENDIX.

The statute is followed by the form of the writ to issue in consequence of it in these words: "Rex vic. salutem:
"Quia coram tali majore vel custode talis villa, vel coram
"custode sigilli nostri de mercatoribus in nundinis in tali
"loco, et tali clerico nostro, A. recognavit debere B.
"tantum quod solvisse debuit tali die, et tali anno, quod
"idem A. nondum solvit, ut dicit: tibi præcipimus quod
"corpus prædicti A. si laicus sit, *capias*, et in prisona nos-
"tra salvo custodiri facias quousque de prædict debito
"satisfecerit. Et qualiter hoc præceptum fueris executus,
"scire facias justiciariis nostris apud Westmonasterium
"per literas tuas sigillatas, et habeas ibi hoc breve.
"Teste, &c."

NOTE I, p. 20.

The first statute against *bailiffs* or *accountants* is the 52 Henry III. c. 23. (stat. of Marlbridge) and is in these words, as in the Cotton M. S. "Provisum est eciam,
"quod se ballivi qui dominis suis compotum reddere te-
"nentur, *se subtraxerint, et terras et tenementa non ha-*
"*buerint*, per que destringi possint; tunc *per eorum corpora*
"attachientur, ita quod vicecomes, in cujus balliva inve-
"niantur, eos venire faciat ad compotum suum redend."

The next statute, here referred to, is the 13 Edw. I. c. 11. (*stat. of Westminster the second*) in these words: "De
"servientibus balivis camerariis et quibuscunque receptori-
"bus qui ad compotum reddendum tenentur concorditer
"est statutum et ordinatum quod cum dominus hujusmodi
"servientium dederit eis auditores compoti et contingat
"ipsos esse in arreragiis super compotum suum *arrestentur*
"*corpora ipsorum*, et per testimonium auditorum ejusdem
"compoti mittantur et liberentur proxime gaole domini
"regis in partibus illis, et a vicecomite seu custode ejus-
"dem gaole recipiantur et mancipentur *carceri in ferris*

"sub

" sub bona custodia, *et in illa prisona remaneant de suo pro-*
" *prio viventes quousque dominus suus de arreragiis plenarie*
" *satisfecerint.*" The statute, however, gave them an appeal from the auditors to the Court of Exchequer, which produced the writ of *ex parte talis—Registrum* 137. F. N. B. 129 f.—And upon giving sureties they were set at liberty till the appeal was discussed, but again committed if found in arrear.

By this statute, and subsequent statutes authorizing imprisonment, process of *outlawry* (which for some time after the conquest took place in cases of felony only) was made competent against the defendant if he fled.

NOTE K, p. 25.

Lord Coke, after commenting upon the destruction of the Jews by the statute de *Judaismo* proceeds with this observation: " At the parliament also of this noble king, " Edward the First, in the 18th year of his reign, another " kind of Jews were severely punished, viz. the judges of " the King's Bench, and of the Common Pleas, the barons " of Exchequer, and the judges itinerant." 2 *Inst.* 506.

The punishment alluded to was for taking bribes in the grossest manner from the parties in every case that occurred.

The contrast afforded by such pictures certainly adds to our relish of the present times.

NOTE L, p. 26.

In the introduction to Crompton's Book of Practice, (p. 52) the concurrent jurisdiction of the Court of King's Bench is thus stated: " In this manner has the Court of " *King's Bench* obtained a concurrent jurisdiction, and
" now

" now holds as it were a *divisum imperium* with the Court
" of *Common Pleas* over all civil actions of a personal, and
" some of a mixt nature. Its *original* jurisdiction we
" have seen of causes between subject and subject, was only
" of such as were of a *tortious* nature, as all *trespasses, res-*
" *cous,* or *pound-breach,* actions of *deceit, conspiracy, forcible*
" *entry, ejectment, replevin,* and *trespass on the case.* Whereas
" its acquired jurisdiction, or rather that jurisdiction which
" is by consequence only, as being founded upon the de-
" fendant's being in the supposed or actual custody of the
" marshal, comprehends all actions of *contract,* whether
" express or implied, *debt, annuity, covenant, account, case*
" for negligence, *nonfeasance, misfeasance,* and *malfea-*
" *sance.*"

The Court of King's Bench proceeds either by *bill,* or upon an *original writ,* from Chancery, at the option of the plaintiff—When upon an original writ, the course of proceeding is exactly the same as that of the Court of Common Pleas—1 Crompton, p. 15.——But there is this material difference between these two modes of commencing the action, that where an action of debt, detinue, covenant, account, case, ejectment, or trespass, is *commenced* in that court (which it is when it proceeds by *bill*) a writ of error lies to a court of appeal instituted by 27 *Eliz.* c. 8. called the *Exchequer Chamber,* consisting of the judges of the Common Pleas and barons of Exchequer; and from thence to the House of Lords—Whereas, if the action proceeded upon an original writ from Chancery, the above statute does not apply, and therefore no writ of error lies to the Court of Exchequer Chamber, but directly to the House of Lords.

NOTE M, p. 28.

This matter is fully stated by Coke, as follows: " The
" Court (of King's Bench) hath power to hold plea by
" *bill* for debt, detinue, covenant, promise, and all other
" personal

"personal actions, *ejectione firmæ*, and the like, against any
"that is in *custodia mareschalli*; or any officer, minister,
"or clerk of the court; and the reason hereof is, that if
"they should be sued in any other court, they should have
"the privilege of this court; and least there should be a
"failure of justice (which is so much abhorred in law)
"they shall be impleaded here by *bill*, though these actions
"be *common pleas*, and are not restrained by the said act of
"Magna Charta, &c." "And all this appeareth by *Brac-*
"*ton*, who lived when Magna Charta was made, *ubi supra*
"where he saith, ' Et aliorum omnium per querelam vel
"' per privilegium, sive libertatem;' and continual expe-
"rience concurreth with antiquity herein."—4 *Inst.* 71.

NOTE N, p. 31.

The 7th of Henry the Fifth, against the makers and publishers of false deeds, is no exception to what is here stated.

NOTE O, p. 34.

The proceedings which were thus supposed are before described, Note E. An original writ for summoning the defendant, with the answer or return to it by the sheriff, appear, however, upon the record of the proceedings as if they had really existed.—The empty form was preserved, and only the substantial operation of the writ thrown aside; because the officers of court, not the legislature, held those proceedings to be unnecessary, in as much as the fees of court could be kept up; though the proceedings were suppressed.

NOTE

NOTE P, p. 37.

It is proper here to observe, that fictions of law are in general so moulded and contrived as to promote the object they profess, viz. " the furtherance of justice:" but it *might* be otherwise; and it is natural to ask, why the legislature should leave the courts to such indirect modes of proceeding? " It is a pity," says that great and venerable judge, *Lord Mansfield*, " that the legislature should be " silent, and force the courts, in order to attain the ends " of justice, to invent legal subtleties, which do not come " up to the common understanding of mankind."— *Douglas*, 523.

" It is repugnant both to the duty and wisdom of law," as *Mr. Eden* (now *Lord Aukland*) observes in his " Principles " of Penal Law," " to seek any ends by the harsh and un- " seemly intervention of subterfuges and fictions. The " candour of legislation should ever be inviolable." P. 197.

The learned author of " *Observations on the Statutes*," observing upon the statute of Henry the Sixth, which makes it competent to meet by contrary evidence the fiction then made use of in the *Marshalsea Court*, that the plaintiff or defendant belonged to the king's houshold, expresses himself thus: " This seems to be a very wise pro- " vision of the legislature, as all such fictions derogate " from the proper weight and dignity in the proceedings " of a court of justice. Use may in some measure have " taken away from the ridicule of the fiction of a *quo minus* " in the Exchequer, as well as other fictions; but the " nature of them cannot be thoroughly altered, so as to " make that proper which in its commencement was a " ridiculous and false surmise." P. 307.

The same author has the following note (p. 94) I still "insist that mystery should always be removed, especi- "ally when no one bad consequence can be suggested "from such a removal." Fabian Phillips, in his Treatise on Capiases and Process of Outlawry, gives this account of the introduction of the *lease* and *release* used by our con- veyancers: "It was first contrived by Serjeant Francis "Moore, at the request of the Lord Norris, to the end that "some of his relations should not know what settlement he "had made." P. 115.

NOTE Q, p. 41.

The stat. 8 Eliz. c. 2, authorizing the judges to give costs and damages in certain cases of vexatious arrests, takes notice of some of the abuses which were then practised in the following preamble: "Whereas divers persons of their "malicious minds, and without any just cause, do many "times cause and procure others of the queen's majesties "loving subjects to be very much molested and troubled "by attachments and arrests made of their bodies, as well "by process of *latitat*, &c. sued out of the court com- "monly called the King's Bench, as also by plaint, bill, &c. "in the court commonly called the Marshalsea, and within "the city of London, and other cities, &c.; and when the "parties that be arrested and attached are brought forth "to answer to such actions and suits as should be objected "against them, then many times there is no declaration or "matter laid against the parties so arrested or attached "whereunto they may make any answer; and so the party "arrested is very maliciously put to great charges and ex- "pences, without any just or reasonable cause; and yet "nevertheless hitherto, by order of the law, the party so "grieved and vexed could never have any costs and da- "mages to him to be judged or awarded for the said unjust
"vexation

" vexation and trouble." The statute, however, after all, left the party wronged to *bring his action* for the recovery of such costs and damages as should be awarded under it.

NOTE R; p. 42.

This statute, 13 Charles II. st. 2. c. 2. is entitled, " An act for prevention of vexations and oppressions by " arrests, and of delays in suits of law." The preamble of it states, " That by the ancient and fundamental laws " of this realm, in case where any person is sued, im-
" pleaded, or arrested by any writ, bill, or process issuing " out of any of his majesty's courts of record at Westmin-
" ster, in any common plea at the suit of any common " person, the *true cause of action* ought to be set forth and " particularly expressed in such writ, bill, or process, " whereby the defendant may have certain knowledge of " the cause of the suit; and the officer who shall execute " such writ, bill, or process, may know how to take se-
" curity for the appearance of the defendant to the same; " and the sureties for such appearance may rightly under-
" stand for what cause they become engaged. *And whereas* " there is great complaint of the people of this realm, that, " for divers years now last past, very many of his majesty's " good subjects have been arrested upon general writs of " *trespass, quare clausum fregit, bill of Middlesex, latitats,* " and other like writs issued out of the Courts of the " King's Bench and Common Pleas, not expressing any " particular or certain cause of action, and thereupon " kept prisoners for a long time for want of bail, *bonds with* " *sureties for appearance having been demanded in so great* " *sums, that few or none have dared to be security for the ap-* " *pearance of such persons so arrested and imprisoned, although* " *in truth there have been little or no cause of action, and*
" oftentimes

" oftentimes there are no such persons who are named plain-
" tiffs; but those arrests have been many times procured by
" malicious persons, to vex and oppress the defendants, or to
" force from them unreasonable or unjust compositions for ob-
" taining their liberty; and by such evil practices many have
" been, and are daily undone, and destroyed in their estates,
" without possibility of having reparation, the actors employed
" in such practices having been (for the most part) poor and
" lurking persons, and their actings so secret, that it hath
" been found very difficult to make true discoveries or proofs
" thereof."

NOTE S, p. 47.

The 12 Geo. I. c. 29, amended by 5 Geo. II. c. 27, and afterwards made perpetual, enacts, "That in all cases where
" the cause of action shall not amount to the sum of *ten pounds*
" or upwards, and the plaintiff or plaintiffs shall proceed by
" way of process against the person, he, she, or they shall
" not arrest or cause to be arrested the body of the defen-
" dant or defendants; but shall serve him, her, or them,
" personally within the jurisdiction of the court, with a copy
" of the process; upon which shall be written an English
" notice to such defendant, of the intent and meaning of
" such service, for which no fee or reward shall be de-
" manded or taken; provided nevertheless, that in parti-
" cular franchises and jurisdictions, the proper officer there
" shall execute such process." It is further enacted,
" That in all cases where the plaintiff's cause of action
" shall amount to the sum of *ten pounds*, or upwards, an
" *affidavit* shall be made and filed of such cause of action;
" which affidavit may be made before any judge or com-
" missioner of the court out of which such process shall
" issue,

" issue, authorized to take such affidavits in such court, or
" else before the officer who shall issue such process, or his
" deputy; which oath such officer, or his deputy, are im-
" powered to administer; and for such affidavit one shil-
" ling, over and above the stamp duties, shall be paid, and
" no more: and the sum or sums specified in such affidavit
" shall be indorsed on the back of such writ or process;
" for which sum or sums so indorsed the sheriff or other
" officer, to whom such writ or process shall be directed,
" shall take bail, and for no more." It is also enacted,
" That if any writ or process shall issue for the sum of *ten*
" *pounds*, or upwards, and *no affidavit* and indorsement
" shall be made as aforesaid, the plaintiff or plaintiffs shall
" not proceed to arrest the body of the defendant or de-
" fendants, but shall proceed in like manner (except as to
" the notice) as is directed in cases where the cause of
" action does not amount to the sum of *ten pounds*, or up-
" wards."

The above is the general law: The direct exceptions to it are those in favour of *volunteer seamen* in his majesty's service, who by 1 Geo. II. c. 14, and subsequent acts, cannot be arrested for a debt under twenty pounds; and of *soldiers*, who have now the same exemption by the annual mutiny acts. There must be an affidavit of debt to the same amount by 11 & 12 W. III. c. 9, before a defendant residing in *Wales* or the *counties palatine* can be held to special bail upon any process issuing out of the courts at Westminster. The courts have also, in practice, imposed as many restrictions upon the arrest of defendants as could be imposed under their authority. These are to be found in the books of practice.

NOTE T, p. 49.

Till within thefe very few years, this execution of the law againſt debtors defcended even to the minuteſt cafes, and fruitleſsly locked up the perfon of the meaneſt labourer. The *Courts of Confcience*, eſtabliſhed by different acts of parliament, who could not arreſt a defendant upon *mefne procefs*, could yet impriſon a debtor *in execution* for the fmalleſt debt; and it appears that creditors were often fo vindictive and abfurd as to keep fuch miferable debtors in prifon for the mereſt trifles. This might appear incredible, if it were not proved by the preamble of a ſtatute fo late as the 25th of his preſent majeſty, c. 45, which is as follows: "Whereas,
" by various acts of parliament now in force, and made
" to eſtabliſh or regulate courts for the recovery of fmall
" debts, particularly in the city of London, &c. there is no
" uniform time limited for the duration of the impriſon-
" ment of a debtor againſt whom an execution, procefs of
" contempt, or precept in the nature of an execution, is
" iſſued, for non-payment of fuch debt and coſts, fum or
" fums of money, as by the order or orders of fuch courts
" fuch debtor or defendant is ordered or directed to pay;
" but fuch debtors and defendants are by fuch acts of par-
" liament to be committed to prifon, there to remain *for*
" *an indefinite length of time*, until he, fhe, or they, ſhall
" perform the order of the court or commiſſioners in that
" behalf; *fo that it frequently happens that a poor perfon,*
" *who is not of ability to pay a debt of or under forty ſhillings,*
" *is impriſoned for many months,* AND SOMETIMES FOR
" YEARS, WITHOUT A POSSIBILITY OF BEING DIS-
" CHARGED."

The ſtatute enacts, That where the debt does not exceed *twenty ſhillings* the debtor ſhall not be confined for more

APPENDIX. 165

more than *twenty days*; and when it does not amount to or exceed *forty shillings*, he shall not be confined for more than *forty days*.

NOTE V, p. 49.

It is the effect of imprisonment in execution, by putting into the hands of the creditor the *person*, to withdraw from him the *estate* of his debtor. To those who are not accustomed to observe this consequence in practice, and to reason upon the principles which give rise to it, this appears a very singular operation of law—and therefore it may not be altogether superfluous here to recite part of the statute of 21 James I. c. 24, which makes the creditor's right to execution against his imprisoned debtor's estate revive upon the debtor's death, if he should die in prison. That statute states the law upon this subject, as follows: " Forasmuch as heretofore it hath been much
" doubted and questioned if any person being in prison,
" and charged in execution, by reason of any judgment
" given against him, should afterwards happen to die in
" execution, whether the party at whose suit, or to whom
" such person stood charged in execution at the time of
" his death, be for ever after concluded and barred to have
" execution of the lands and goods of such person so
" dying—*And forasmuch as daily experience doth manifest*
" *that divers persons, of sufficiency in real and personal estate,*
" *minding to deceive others of their just debts, for which they*
" *stood charged in execution, have obstinately and wilfully*
" *chosen rather to live and die in prison than to make any*
" *satisfaction according to their abilities*; To prevent which
" deceit, and for the avoiding of such doubts and questions
" hereafter, Be it declared, explained, and enacted, &c.

" that

"that from and after the end of the present session of parliament the party or parties at whose suit, or to whom
any person shall stand charged in execution for any debt
or damages recovered, his or their executors or administrators, may, after the death of the said person so charged and dying in execution, lawfully sue forth and have
new execution against the lands and tenements, goods
and chattels, or any of them, of the person so deceased,
in such manner and form, to all intents and purposes, as
he or they, or any of them, might have had by the laws
and statutes of this realm, if such person so deceased had
never been taken or charged in execution."—But this
statute left the law as it was with regard to the debtor's
estate during his life, nor has it yet been altered. The
debtor's imprisonment protects his estate from the execution of all those creditors at whose suit he is imprisoned or
detained.

NOTE U, p. 49.

A short deduction shall here be given of the law of
arrest and execution against the person, or of civil imprisonment, in *Scotland*:

In that country, where the laws are in some respects
justly, but in others erroneously, supposed to bear harder
upon the private rights of individuals than in England, no
arrest of the person of a mere *defendant*, as the effect of ordinary process in an action, is or ever was suffered to take
place. The plaintiff, however, has it in his power to attach, by *arrestment*, the money and effects of the defendant
in the hands of third persons, till he give bail, or *find
caution* to the amount of the arrestment, as a security for
the sums which the plaintiff may eventually be entitled to
recover upon the decree or judgment. He may also, by
serving

serving upon him, and publishing a writ called an *Inhibition*, disable him from aliening his lands or real estate pending the action, and obtain a security over them to answer the event. But if it be made appear to the *Court of Session* (the supreme civil court) that it is intended vexatiously or maliciously, they will stop the inhibition. These are the preventive measures which in Scotland stand in place of the arrest and imprisonment of defendants.

But in certain special cases there are summary arrests for civil causes. A foreigner may be so arrested for a debt due to an inhabitant of the country till he find bail. 1 *Bankton*, 461.—And upon the oath of a creditor, stating his debt, and that he has reason to think his debtor is in *meditatione fugæ*, intending to withdraw suddenly from the kingdom, in order to disappoint his creditors, a warrant will immediately issue for arresting and imprisoning him till he find caution *judicio sisti* (*i. e.*) to appear in court. But the person so arrested will recover heavy damages if it appear that the arrest was without good reason; and the creditor may be obliged to give security to that effect. By special act of parliament (1672, c. 8) restrictive and correctory of former practice, " a " merchant" (which also means shopkeeper and retail dealer) " innkeeper, or stabler," within a royal borough may arrest a stranger who resides without the borough, for articles furnished to him in the proper course of the creditor's dealing, till he give security to appear in the court of the borough; provided such merchant, &c. has no other security for the debt than his own books. *Border* warrants, which take place on the border between England and Scotland, also afford instances of summary arrest in Scotland.

Anciently there was in Scotland no execution against the person of a debtor. It was not a natural idea that there should be any such execution: and the same principles which rendered it long inadmissible in England had the same effect in Scotland.

APPENDIX.

In the reign of *Alexander* the Second, and he began to reign in the year 1214, the law of execution for debt was settled or declared by the following statute:

" If the debtor, or his tenants, has moveable goods, first
" of all they shall be distrained for payment of the debt to
" the creditor.

2. " And if they have no distrainable goods, the sheriff
" and the king's servants, before the court rise, shall adver-
" tise the debtor that for inlaik (defect) of moveable goods,
" they are bound by the law to sell his lands and possessions
" to satisfy the creditor within fifteen days.

3. " The debtor not doing this within fifteen days, the
" sheriff and the king's servants shall sell the lands and
" possessions pertaining to the debtor, *conform to the con-*
" *suetude of the realm*, until the creditor be satisfied of
" the principal sum, with damage, expences, and interest.

4. " And if the lands are holden of the king, the sheriff
" shall infeft the buyer, by ane precept, who buys them.

5. " And if they be holden of ane baron, and he would
" buy them, by the law he should have them.

6. " And if another man will take them upon the king's
" price, the sheriff shall infeft him in such form as the
" debtor possessed them, with all his rights and pertinents
" whatsomever.

7. " And at command of the sheriff the baron shall re-
" ceive the buyer to be his tenant, and shall give him such
" possession as the debtor had, without any question or im-
" pediment."

Thus stood the creditor's right of execution in Scotland in the beginning of the thirteenth century.

In the beginning of the fourteenth century the right of execution against the *persons* of debtors was introduced in favour of *merchants*, by a statute merchant for Scotland, of the same import, in that respect, with the statute merchant which had passed some little time before in England. This was by the 2 stat. of *Robert* the First, c. 19. It is entitled

" *anent*

"anent payment of merchants debts." And the first section of it is in these words: "If ane merchant has proved his
" debt owing to him, by an assize, or by any other man-
" ner, the mayor or alderman of the town, or the keeper
" of the village, shall take and apprehend the debtor, if
" he be ane laick man, wherever he may find him within
" his jurisdiction, and deliver him to the prison of the
" town, if he has ane prison; and there the debtor shall
" remain upon his own proper expences until he satisfy
" and pay the debt: and command shall be given to the
" keeper of the prison of the town, that he receive him at
" the command of the mayor, or of the alderman. And if
" the jaylor receive him he shall answer for the debt, if he
" has so much in goods and geir."

Section 4. " If the debtor cannot find the way to pay
" the debt, the mayor or the jaylor, under his seal, shall
" certify the king's chancellor of the quantity and clear-
" ness of the debt, within ane quarter of ane year after
" the debtor was taken. And the moveable goods, and
" the lands pertaining to the debtor, shall be taken, com-
" prised, and given for payment of the debt.

5. " And *if his goods are not sufficient* for payment of
" the debt, his body shall remain in prison until all the
" debt be paid, and the creditor shall find to him bread
" and water."

This statute contains many o her provisions respecting the debtor's estate and the creditor's security.

Soon after, a writ came in practice to be issued *at common law* against every person who had become bound to do any specific act *(ad factum præstandum,* as it was technically expressed) by which he was ordered, in name of the king, to fulfil his obligation, or " surrender his person in
" ward," that is, go to prison; on pain of being declared a *rebel.*—And, afterwards, by act of parliament, 1584, c. 139, ratifying an *act of sederunt* (i. e.) a general rule of
the

the Court of Session, made two years before, a writ was authorized, by which all debtors in sums of money ascertained by judgment were commanded to pay, on pain of rebellion: and if they were declared or denounced rebels, a writ issued for seizing and imprisoning their persons. Upon this footing the law of personal execution was further extended and regulated by *various acts of parliament, and of sederunt*, till it came to be fixed and established.

Execution against the person, as thus established, proceeds either upon the decree or judgment of a competent court—or a regular bond, or written obligation, containing a clause of consent that such execution shall issue, and made a record of court by registration—or, upon a bill of exchange or promissory note, duly protested, and also made a record of court by registration. The exemplification, or *extract*, as it is called, upon such registration, either implies or contains a precept or warrant for execution.

The precepts or warrants of inferior courts, however, do not (with one exception) of themselves authorize imprisonment. They only authorize the proper officer to *charge* or command the debtor to pay within a certain number of days; after which his effects, within the jurisdiction of the court from which the warrant issues, can be *poinded* (i. e.) seized and delivered to the creditor, by appraisement, towards satisfaction of the debt.

The exception above alluded to respects the precepts of the magistrates of royal boroughs, who can imprison the debtor upon what is called an *act of warding*, if he fail to pay after the time allowed to him by the precept for paying the debt is elapsed. Of this privilege the magistrates of royal boroughs have been long in possession. It is with reason supposed to be the remains, in practice, of the *statute merchant*.

In all other cases of execution, the imprisonment of the debtor proceeds upon writs or warrants which issue from the Court of Session;—the nature and course of which may be very shortly stated.

Letters

Letters of *horning*, as they are termed, (for a reason which will appear in the sequel) are the writs which must first issue and run their course, before imprisonment in execution can take place. They proceed, of course, upon the decrees or judgments of the Court of Session, or upon the written instruments already mentioned, when registered in that court; and they also proceed upon the decrees or judgments of inferior courts, or such written instruments registered in such inferior courts; but not till warrants are obtained from the Court of Session, authorizing the execution. Such warrants are granted of course, upon production of the precepts of the inferior court, after the expiration of the *induciæ* allowed to the debtors by such precepts.

The writ thus issuing under the authority of the Court of Session is of the nature which has already been generally mentioned, viz. a command in the king's name, to do the thing or pay the money which the judgment or precept of the court ordered the person against whom it issued to do or to pay, within a certain number of days (which is different in different cases, but in no case, unless when the debtor resides in Orkney or Shetland, does it exceed *fifteen* days) " under the pain of rebellion, *and putting him to the horn*." It also contains a warrant for *poinding* the debtor's effects. A civil rebellion is the legal consequence of his failing to obey this writ; and unless he shew good cause to the Court of Session why he should not obey it, by a *bill of suspension*, that is, a petition to have the execution suspended, he is declared a *rebel* at the Market Cross of Edinburgh, or of the head borough of the district wherein he resides. This is supposed to be done with great solemnity, by proclamation of *Oyeses*, and blast of *horn*.—The horn was the trumpet of simple times.

When the debtor has been proclaimed or " *denounced*" a rebel, and put to the horn by virtue of the letters of horning, which appears by the return of the proper officer upon the writ; and when the horning, and the service of it with

the

the "denunciation," have been recorded in a special register appointed for that purpose, another summary application is made to the Court of Session, and *letters of caption* or *capias* issue of course. By this writ the king commands his sheriffs and messengers to " search for and apprehend" the debtor, and put him in prison, there to remain on his own expences till he obey the command of the former letters or writ; that is, till he do the thing or pay the debt required. Upon this writ, which contains a warrant to break open locks and doors in executing it, he may be immediately seized and imprisoned, wherever he can be found within Scotland.

These writs of horning and caption, with all other warrants of execution authorized by the Court of Session, pass the royal signet, being first signed by one of the *clerks* or *writers to his majesty's signet*—a respectable body of men, whose *official* functions, privileges, and rank in the law of Scotland, cannot be described by any thing analogous to them in England.

A person imprisoned by letters of *caption* under the authority of the Court of Session, and of his majesty's signet, as already described, may be set at liberty, according to modern practice, upon the discharge or acquittance of his creditor or creditors so imprisoning or detaining him: but there are other modes in which he may by law regain his liberty—and these are now to be shortly stated.

A *bill of suspension* has been already described as a petition to the Court of Session, shewing cause why execution upon a decree or precept ought to be stayed or suspended. This bill or petition is also signed by a clerk or writer to the signet, as the writs of execution are so signed; and if the desire of the petition is granted, a writ called *letters of suspension* is issued under the signet, and signed in the same manner, commanding all officers of the law to desist from putting the decree or judgment or precept in execution.

tion. But such letters staying execution, which, in spite of every attention in the power of the judges, are productive of much delay and vexation to just creditors, cannot, in the general case, pass till caution or bail is found for the amount of the sum in dispute, and of such costs or damages as may afterwards be awarded by the court, in case the execution shall ultimately be ordered to proceed—the sufficiency of the bail or caution being approved by an officer of court, whose business it is to make the necessary enquiries, and who is responsible for the discharge of his duty. If the debtor cannot give sufficient caution, he must make oath that it is the best he can give, and at the same time execute a disposition or conveyance *omnium bonorum* as a further security. This is technically called *juratory caution*.

The proceeding by suspension usually takes place where the debtor thinks he has grounds for it, *before* he is imprisoned: but even after he is so imprisoned he may apply to the Court of Session by a similar bill or petition for having the execution suspended, with an additional prayer to discharge him out of custody while the matter is in dependence. This, when passed, is called a *suspension and liberation*, and is not passed without much precaution and deliberation.

A civil debtor in prison, who makes oath that he is not able to defray the expence of his subsistence, may be discharged out of prison by the judge or magistrate of the jurisdiction, unless the creditor at whose suit he is in prison agree, within ten days after a petition has been served upon him, to pay his debtor for subsistence not under *three pence a day*. This is by a special act of parliament (1696, c. 32.) which has been called *an act of grace*. Its operation is not restricted to the case of debtors within a certain amount, nor does it afford any future protection either to the person or estate of the debtor; but he is entitled to his action for

damages,

damages, if he is imprisoned by the creditor for the same debt without any new reason for so doing; that is, if he is so imprisoned oppressively.

But the general remedy in Scotland to *all* debtors who are imprisoned for civil debts which they cannot pay, and who have not been guilty of fraud, is the action of *cessio bonorum*; a proceeding which has its imperfections, but is founded upon a just and rational principle.

The action of *cessio bonorum* is a very ancient common law remedy. It proceeds upon the principle, in Scotch law, that the sole purpose of imprisonment is to force the debtor, *squalore carceris*, to give every satisfaction in his power, or make a full discovery of his effects. Imprisonment for debt is not there considered either as a punishment or a satisfaction, but as affording means which may lead to both.

The law declares, therefore, that an imprisoned debtor who has committed no fraud, and has no effects to deliver up, or is willing to discover all that he has, is entitled to his discharge: and yet that in certain cases, even without fraud, he is liable to punishment.

When a debtor has been one month in prison he may bring his action of *cessio bonorum* before the Court of Session, which states the cause of his insolvency, and his readiness to deliver up all his effects, and, having made his creditors parties, demands his release, as matter of common right. " He
" must exhibit upon oath a particular inventory of his
" estate, and depose that he has neither heritage nor move-
" ables, other than is contained in that inventory, and that
" he hath made no conveyance of any part thereof, since
" his imprisonment, to the prejudice of his creditors: he
" must also declare upon oath whether he hath made any
" such conveyance before his imprisonment, and point out
" the persons to whom, and the cause of granting it, that the
" court may judge whether he has by any fraudulent or col-
" lusive practice forfeited his claim to liberty; and he must
" make

APPENDIX. 175

"make over to his creditors the whole of his estate abso-
"lutely, and without the least reservation."

If any thing fraudulent appear against him, he is considered as one who has "forfeited his claim to liberty," and is denied the benefit of the action. But if no fraud appear, and if he deliver up his effects, and in all other respects conform himself to the rules and orders of court, a decree is pronounced in his favour, and he is discharged out of custody.

The effect of this decree is as follows—

With regard to his *person*, it frees him from future imprisonment for debts then due to those creditors whom he made parties to the action. Those who had not an opportunity of opposing the decree are not bound by it.

With regard to his *estate*, future acquisitions are not protected by it: they are liable to the creditor's execution as if there had been no such proceeding; with the reservation only, out of such future estate, of a *beneficium competentiæ*, that is, as much as the court shall think necessary for the debtor's subsistence.

And with regard to his *reputation*, the decree of *cessio* was formerly made to carry along with it circumstances of disgrace to the person who obtained it, which it is impossible to reconcile with the ideas and principles on which it proceeded. Although the insolvent could not obtain it if he had been guilty of any thing fraudulent, or without discovering and giving up his effects, yet by *act of sederunt*, or general rule of the Court of Session, May 17, 1606, a pillory was ordered to be erected at the Market Cross of Edinburgh, with a seat upon it, where all such insolvents discharged by *cessio bonorum* were once to be exposed, on a market day at noon, with a hat or bonnet of yellow colour, to be worn constantly by them, under the pain of three months imprisonment if apprehended at any time without it: and in the year 1669 another *act of sederunt* was made upon this subject,

ject, in these words: "The lords ordain that in all de-
"creets of *bonorum* to be decerned hereafter, there be an
"express clause insert, ordaining the party in whose fa-
"vour the *bonorum* is granted to wear the habit of *bankrupt*,
"and that they take on the habit before they come out
"(of prison) and come out therewith; and that it shall be
"lawful and free to their creditors to seize and imprison
"any of them whenever they shall be found wanting the
"habit upon them. And the lords declare that the habit
"is to be a coat or upper garment, which is to cover their
"clothes, body, and arms, whereof the one half is to be
"of a yellow, and the other half of a brown colour, and a
"cap or hood which they are to wear on their head, as
"said is."

It is remarkable that this permanent mark of disgrace
was thus to be inflicted indiscriminately upon all insolvents,
or, as they were technically termed, *dyvours*, or bankrupts,
discharged by *cessio bonorum*; but a severity so rigorous, and
often so preposterous and unjust, could not fail in time to correct itself. Accordingly about twenty years after, the Lords
of Session declared, indirectly, by another *act of federunt*,
(July 18, 1688) that they would dispense with the party-
coloured habit in cases of insolvency through mere misfortune; but by act of parliament 1696, c. 5, they were
prohibited from dispensing with it in any other case, and
unless such misfortunes were clearly alledged and proved.—
This continues to be the law at this day; and although it is
now hardly ever put in practice, yet there have been some
instances, but a few years back, where the Court of Session
have refused to dispense with the habit.

The result of the whole is, that in Scotland no *defendant*
is in the ordinary course of process liable to arrest: that no
debtor can be arrested or imprisoned in execution without a
previous *charge* or notice, by service of a writ ordering him
to pay within a certain number of days: that upon the expiration

piration of that time, if he has not obtained a stay of execution, upon cause shewn, and bail or caution given, he may upon another writ or capias be immediately arrested and imprisoned: that, if he is so arrested unjustly, he may, upon good cause shewn, obtain his release by a suspension and liberation: that if he has no cause to shew against the debt or proceedings, but yet has done nothing fraudulent, he is certain of regaining his liberty by the action of *cessio bonorum*; while his creditors, who are made parties, lose nothing but the power of again putting him in prison: that although he has done nothing directly fraudulent, yet if his insolvency has not arisen from mere misfortunes, as, for example, if it has arisen from gross extravagance, or from losses in the course of an illicit trade, the insolvent or bankrupt (for these words are on this subject used synonymously) may be exposed to public reproach, by being obliged to wear a party-coloured habit: and that if he has done any thing fraudulent, he is considered as one who has forfeited his claim to liberty.

It need hardly be added, that as civil imprisonment in Scotland is only for the purpose of discovery and coercion, and is not considered in any sense as a satisfaction, a creditor who has imprisoned his debtor is not thereby deprived of his right of execution against his estate or effects. Whatever may have been the case anciently (for the learned *Craig* has said that the law was different in his time, but was soon altered) it has for these two last centuries been the law of Scotland that the creditor can resort to execution against his imprisoned debtor's lands and goods, as a concurrent remedy.

By the laws of *Holland* no *defendant* can, as such, be arrested on process in the action. A *debtor* only, after

after judgment obtained against him, may be imprisoned. But he has the action of *cessio bonorum*, by which an honest insolvent debtor regains his liberty, as in Scotland—And the laws of some of the great trading cities of *Germany* are nearly the same.

NOTE W, p. 53.

The *Marquis of Beccaria*, in his Essay on Crimes and Punishments, treating of the imprisonment of a person who by *misfortune* has been deprived of the means of paying his debts, expresses himself thus: " Why is he ranked " with criminals, and, in despair, compelled to repent of " his honesty? Conscious of his innocence he lived easy " and happy under the protection of those laws which, it is " true, he violated, but not intentionally; laws dictated " by the avarice of the rich, and accepted by the poor, " seduced by that universal flattering hope which makes " men believe that all unlucky accidents are the lot of " others, and the most fortunate only their share. Mankind, when influenced by the first impressions, love cruel " laws, although, being subject to them themselves, it is " the interest of every person that they should be as mild " as possible; but the fear of being injured is always " more prevalent than the intention of injuring others."— Chap. 34.

APPENDIX.

NOTE X, p. 59.

The practice of the Court of *Common Pleas* is different from that of the Court of *King's Bench* in receiving affidavits of debt to hold to bail. In the Court of Common Pleas the defendant may file a cross affidavit, and then the plaintiff may file an additional one in supplement of the former; consequently it is not thought necessary that the affidavit should be so positive in the Court of Common Pleas as in the Court of King's Bench.——See 1 *Term Reports*, 716.

NOTE Y, p. 63.

Puffendorff, as translated by *Barbeyrac*, expresses himself upon this subject as follows: " Car comme l'avenir est in-
" certain par rapport aux hommes, et q'ainsi il peut arri-
" ver, ou que nos forces diminuent par quelque accident
" imprevu, ou q'une revolution soudaine nous fasse per-
" dre l'occasion d'agir, ou nous la rende du moins
" plus difficile a trouver; comme d'ailleurs toute le péné-
" tration du monde n'empêche pas que l'on ne se trompe
" souvent dans l'examen de ses propres forces, et des diffi-
" cultés de la chose a quoi l'on s'engage : on doit toujours
" presumer que les contractans n'ont jamais perdu de vue
" la foiblesse de la nature humaine, et q'ainsi en determi-
" nant ce qu'ils devoient faire a l'avenir les uns pour les au-
" tres, ils ont supposé, comme une condition tacite, que leur
" forces, et l'occasion d'agir, demeurassent au même état,
" ou

" ou qu'ils n'eussent pas conçu une trop haute idée de
" leur pouvoir présent. *En ces cas la, on a raison de dire,*
" *que celui qui fait tout ce qui depend de lui, remplit exacte-*
" *ment son devoir;* sur tout si, dans l'execution même,
" il survient quelque obstacle invincible qui en empêche
" l'effet, ou qui le detourne ailleurs."—*Puffendorff de Jure
Gentium et Naturæ,* traduit par Barbeyrac, lib 3, c. 7, § 4.

Barbeyrac's translation is quoted, because the translator is himself an authority, as well as a commentator upon his author.

NOTE Z, p. 63.

We have the authority of the *legislature* to say, that insolvency is legally consistent with honesty.—The preamble to the 22 & 23 Car. II. c. 20. is in the following words:
" Forasmuch as very many persons now detained in prison
" are miserably impoverished, either by reason of *the late*
" *unhappy times, the sad and dreadful fire, their own mis-*
" *fortunes,* or otherwise, so as they *are totally disabled to*
" *give any satisfaction to their creditors,* and so become,
" *without advantage to any,* a charge and burden to the
" kingdom, and by noisomeness (inseparably incident to
" extreme poverty) may become the occasion of pestilence
" and contagious diseases, to the great prejudice of the
" kingdom," &c. And section 13 of that act, after stating the practice of lodging debtors and felons in one room and bed, goes on thus: " Whereby many times *honest*
" *gentlemen,* tradesmen, and others, *prisoners for debt,* are
" *disturbed,*" &c.

NOTE

NOTE A A, p. 66.

If it were not the general idea, fortified by authority, that *punishment* is a leading principle of the present law of imprisonment for debt, so much should not have been said to shew that it is utterly inconsistent in all its parts with the principle of punishment; more especially as the matter seems to be decided by Lord Coke, in the following passage: " A man in prison by process of law ought to be kept in " *salva et arcta custodia*, and by the law ought not to go " out, though it be with a keeper, and with the leave and " sufferance of the gaoler; but yet imprisonment must be " *custodia et non pæna*, for (speaking of civil imprison- " ment) *Carcer ad homines custodiendos, non ad puniendos* " *dari debet*." 1 Inst. 260.

And the idea of imprisonment for debt being for the purpose of coercion by means of close confinement, seems to have been sufficiently established in the reign of Richard the Second, by a statute for the purpose of preventing prisoners for debt from being suffered to go at large, and thereby enjoying " greater *sweet* of prison," as it is whimsically enough expressed, than they ought to have. By that statute (1 Richard II. c. 12.) " It is," among other things, " ordained, that if any, at the suit of the party judged to " another prison for debt, trespass, or other quarrel, will " confess himself voluntarily, and by a feigned cause debtor " to the King; and by that means to be judged to the said " prison of the *Fleet*, there *to have greater sweet of prison* " than elsewhere, and so to delay the party of his recovery; " the same recognizance shall be there received, and if he be " not debtor to the King of record, his body shall inconti- " nently be remanded to the prison where he was before,

" there

" there to remain till he hath made gree (tan qil avera fait
" gree) to the said party, and, the same gree made, he shall
" immediately be sent again to the *Fleet*, there to abide till
" he hath made gree to the King of his recognizance
" aforesaid."

NOTE BB, p. 70.

It is wonderful that misers do not more frequently contract debts, purchase lands or goods, and then provoke imprisonment: for the chief enjoyment of avarice arises from that sort of self-gratulation which the reflections of a miser suggest, when he compares his own abundant *means*, with the wants of the wretched or improvident around him; and as nothing but fear can restrain him from acts of villainy for the increase of that store which is the basis of his ideal superiority, a voluntary imprisonment would, to such a man, be a safe and profitable species of robbery. He could not be hanged; his acquisitions would be secured to him for life; and his place of residence might afford him the best possible opportunities of relishing the poverty of others. In fact, many such instances did occur before the statute of *James the First* (already stated in note N) as appears from the preamble of the second section, in these words:
" *And forasmuch as daily experience doth manifest that divers*
" *persons of sufficiency in real and personal estate, minding to*
" *deceive others of their just debts, for which they stood charged*
" *in execution, have obstinately and wilfully chosen rather to*
" *live and die in prison than to make any satisfaction according to their abilities.*"—And as that statute only restored to the creditor his right of execution against the debtor's estate if he died in prison, such instances as are there described have since, not unfrequently, occurred; to the
amazement

amazement of unprofeffional men, who cannot conceive from what caufe or principle fo ftrange a confequence fhould follow.

This arifes from the pofition in law, ftated in general p. 61, and confidered in the chapter now referred to, that imprifonment in execution is of itfelf a fatisfaction to the creditor. Sir William Blackftone has faid that " the " confinement of the debtor's body" is confidered in law as even " an *ample* fatisfaction to the creditor," and " that " the confinement is the whole of the debtor's punifh- " ment, and of the fatisfaction made to the creditor." Nor can this fort of execution require, or indeed, upon the above principle, admit of fupplementary aid by means of any other; fo that although it may be reforted to for the purpofe of making up for the defects or inefficacy of other modes of execution, it has been fhewn that no other mode of execution can come in aid of it. The maxim on this fubject has been, *corpus humanum non recipit æftimationem*.

The books of practice ftate this remarkable part of the law thus: " An *elegit*" (that is, an execution againft the debtor's lands) " may be had after a *fieri facias*" (that is, an execution againft his goods.) " But *if once the body* " *is taken* there cannot be a *fieri facias*, or *elegit*; *for the* " *body is deemed the higheft fatisfaction the plaintiff can* " *have.*"——" If you *firft* fue out a *fieri facias* againft " the defendant's goods, and levy part thereof, you may " afterwards have a *capias ad fatisfaciendum* againft his " body for the refidue, or a fecond *fieri facias* or an *elegit* " for the refidue; but if you *firft* imprifon upon a *capias* " *ad fatisfaciendum*, you cannot have a *fieri facias* or an " *elegit.*"

So completely is it eftablifhed that imprifonment in execution is a full and ample fatisfaction to the creditor: and accordingly many diftinctions will be found in the books, in cafes of *efcapes*, which are intelligible upon that principle only.

NOTE CC, p. 72.

Barbeyrac, in a note upon Puffendorff, expresses himself on this subject thus: " On avoit crû que chez les Romains, " une loi de 12 tables permettoit aux créanciers de mettre " en pieces le corps de leur debiteur, et de le partager entre " eux; et cette opinion etoit même appuiée sur l'autorité " de *Quinctilian*, Inst. Orat. lib. 3. c. 6, *d'Aulu Gelle*, *Noct*. " *Att*. lib. 20. c. 1, et de *Tertullian*, *Apologet*. cap. 4. " Mais Monsieur de *Bynkershock* vient de prouver evidem- " ment, dans ses *Observations*, lib. 1. c. 1. qu'il s'agit la " seulement d'une vente de la personne même du debiteur, " faite par voie d'encan." Lib. 3. c. 7. n. 7.

The law and practice of the Romans respecting debtors were indeed sufficiently cruel and barbarous, without any such hideous and absurd brutality as has been ascribed by certain authors to that extraordinary people. In the early ages of the republic, and before the introduction of the *cessio bonorum*, the person of the debtor was the property of his creditor, who either sold him as a common slave, or confined him in *privato carcere*; whipping and torturing him occasionally, either for the purpose of making him discover effects, or of gratifying a savage resentment.

NOTE DD, p. 72.

Were it necessary to prove that this is not speculation unsupported by fact—that while it is certain there are many debtors who deserve the utmost severity of law, there are also many creditors who persist, with the most absurd and unfeeling obstinacy, in confining debtors who

have

have evidently failed through misfortune, and are abfolutely unable to difcharge their debts — were it neceffary to prove this by facts, the multitude of debtors who were thrown into prifon after the great fire of London, many of whom had loft their all, and been rendered infolvent by that great calamity, and who were neverthelefs kept in gaol, and the moft wretched mifery, by their brutal creditors, would afford fufficient evidence to fupport the affertion, that fuch things do very frequently happen. The fact alluded to is known hiftorically, and proved by the preamble of the 22 & 23 Car. II. c. 20.

Nay repeated inftances have occurred, even of late, where creditors perfifted in keeping the body of a debtor in gaol after the mind was gone, that is, after he had become *infane*.—And the courts have been obliged to refufe (certainly with reluctance) to difcharge debtors who were admitted to be in that miferable fituation. See *Kernot* againft *Norman*, 2 *Term Rep.* 390.—There are even inftances of perfons arrefted when in a ftate of infanity; and the Court of King's Bench was under the neceffity of refufing an application laft Michaelmas term to difcharge a man whom his creditor, knowing him to be infane, had fo arrefted, and ftill kept in prifon, though raving mad, as a debtor in execution.

Were further evidence yet neceffary, it might be found in the proceedings of a charitable fociety to be particularly noticed in the fequel.

NOTE EE, p. 74.

A very ingenious man and philofophic lawyer, obferving upon the *litis conteftatio* of the Romans, after mentioning that it ceafed to be a judicial contract, goes on in thefe words: " But then it was defined to be a *quafi* contract, " which,

"which, in plain language, is saying, that it hath nothing
"of a contract except the name."

Lord Kaims's Law Tracts, 296.

NOTE F F, p. 85.

Without meaning to adopt the following opinion of *Puffendorff*, it may be of some use to contrast it with the arguments quoted in this chapter from Sir William Blackstone. "Confiderandum preterea hic eft, quam quis
"caufam aut necessitatem habuerit debitum contrahendi.
"Prout enim hæc gravis aut levis fuerit, favor debitoris
"inopis aut miferatio intenditur aut remittitur. Unde
"recte duriore habentur conditione *mercatores*, etiam qui
"per cafum fortuitum folvendo effe defierunt, quam alii
"qui ex peculiari quadam neceffitate pecunias mutuo fu-
"mere funt adacti. Illos enim lucri cupido debita con-
"trahere fubigit. Et cum ipfi artem ditefcendi profitean-
"tur vix culpa carent qui etiam fortuito non præcaverunt;
"puta, qui omnes fuas fortunas uni cafui expofuerunt."

Puff. de Jure Nat. et Gentium, lib. 3. c. 7. § 3.

Sir William Blackftone's Commentaries have been particularly referred to, becaufe that work is not confined to the collections of lawyers, but juftly holds a diftinguifhed place in the library of every gentleman. It is an authority, therefore, which can be consulted by every body.

APPENDIX.

NOTE GG, p. 88.

The application of this principle in the bankrupt laws perhaps requires correction. The object of it is, that deserving men, who have suffered by innocent errors and misfortunes in trade, shall be protected, and preserved to their country; but that deserving men *only*, (as far as law can distinguish that character) shall be so protected. The objection is, that the law does not discriminate so much as it might: that provided a man has sufficient address to procure a concurrence of four-fifths of his creditors, and no *direct* act of fraud appear against him, he may receive the protection of the bankrupt law in its fullest extent (if no objection is stated to the lord chancellor) although he has been all along playing at hazard in trade, with the money of others, and wilfully exposing them to the utmost jeopardy, merely to purchase to himself a very remote chance of gain, or immediate support in a line many degrees above his fair pretensions. This, it must be confessed, is a delicate subject, and too many conditions might defeat one great object of the law; but surely, upon the same principle that *gaming* to a certain extent, or giving a certain sum of money to a daughter upon her marriage, are circumstances which by the statute exclude the bankrupt from all benefit under it; others still more prevalent, in that line of life, might be added. Were there more precaution in that respect, so as to place in the situation of common insolvents those bankrupt traders who have been guilty of certain mal-practices which admit of definition, there would not be so much room for the reflection, that the bankrupt law is much less resorted to for the benefit of creditors than for that of debtors—and men of integrity would be less frequently shocked at the unprincipled arrogance of those stately bankrupts who are to be seen in all the public walks of trade, looking down upon their indigent creditors, and grown great by dishonesty.

NOTE

NOTE HH, p. 111.

That part of the Lords Act which relates to the dif‑
charge of the prisoner, after having directed the manner of
his being brought up, the oath he is to take, and the assign‑
ment and conveyance he is to execute in favour of his
creditors, proceeds (section 13) in these words: " And
" upon every such assignment and conveyance being exe‑
" cuted by any such prisoner or prisoners, he, she, or they
" shall be discharged out of custody by rule or order
" of such court, which shall be petitioned by any such
" prisoner; and such rule or order being produced to, and
" a copy thereof being left with, any such sheriff, gaoler,
" or keeper of any prison as aforesaid, shall be a sufficient
" warrant to him to discharge and set at liberty forthwith
" every such prisoner and prisoners, who shall be ordered as
" aforesaid to be discharged, without taking any fee, or
" detaining him, her, or them, in respect of any demand
" of any such sheriff, warden, marshal, gaoler, or keeper,
" for or in respect of chamber rent or lodging, or other‑
" wise, or for or in respect of any fees theretofore claim‑
" ed or due to any such sheriff, &c. or any employed by
" or under him or them; and no such sheriff, &c. shall
" afterwards be liable to any action of escape, or other suit
" or information on that account, or for what he shall do
" in pursuance of this act; and the person or persons to
" whom the estate and effects of any such prisoner or
" prisoners shall be assigned and conveyed, shall, with all
" convenient speed, sell and dispose of the estates and effects
" of every such prisoner which shall be so assigned and
" conveyed; and shall divide the nett produce of all such
" estates and effects *among the creditors of every such pri‑*
" *soner and prisoners, if more than one, who shall have*
" *charged*

APPENDIX. 189

" *charged every such prisoner in execution, before the time of*
" *such prisoner's petition to be discharged shall have been pre-*
" *sented,* rateably and in proportion to their respective
" debts; but in case the person or persons at whose suit
" any such prisoner or prisoners stood charged in execution
" as aforesaid *shall not be satisfied with the truth of any*
" *such prisoner's oath*; and shall either personally, or by his,
" her, or their attorney, if he, she, or they cannot per-
" sonally attend, and proof shall be made thereof to the
" satisfaction of any such court as aforesaid, desire further
" time to inform him, her, or themselves, of the matters
" contained therein, *any such court may remand any such*
" *prisoner or prisoners, and direct him, her, or them, and*
" *the person or persons dissatisfied as aforesaid with such oath,*
" *to appear either in person, or by his, her, or their attorney,*
" *on some other day,* to be appointed by such said court,
" some time at furthest within the first week of the term
" next following the time of such examination, but sooner
" if any such court shall so think fit; and all objections
" which shall be made as to the insufficiency in point of
" form against any prisoner's schedule of his estates and
" effects, shall be only made the first time any such pri-
" soner shall be brought up; and if at such second day
" which shall be appointed the creditor or creditors dissa-
" tisfied with such oath shall make default in appearing,
" either in person, or by his, her, or their attorney; or in
" case he, she, or they shall appear, *if he, she, or they*
" *shall be unable to discover any estate or effects of the prisoner*
" *omitted in the account set forth in such his or her petition,*
" then and in any such case such court shall, by rule or
" order thereof, immediately *cause the said prisoner or pri-*
" *soners to be discharged,* upon such prisoner or prisoners exe-
" cuting such assignment and conveyance of his or her estates
" and effects in manner as assignments and conveyances
" of prisoners estates and effects are hereinbefore directed
" to be made, UNLESS *such creditor or creditors who shall*
" *have*

" *have charged any such prisoner in execution as aforesaid,*
" *his, her, or their executors or administrators,* DOTH OR DO
" INSIST UPON SUCH PRISONER OR PRISONERS BE-
" ING DETAINED IN PRISON, and shall agree, by wri-
" ing signed with his, her, or their name or names, mark
" or marks, or under the hand of his, her, or their attor-
" ney, in case any such creditor or creditors, his, her, or
" their executors or administrators, shall be out of England,
" *to pay and allow weekly a sum not exceeding two shillings*
" *and four pence, as any such court shall think fit, unto the*
" *said prisoner, to be paid every Monday in every week, so*
" *long as any such prisoner shall continue in prison in execu-*
" *cution at the suit of any such creditor or creditors; and in every*
" *such case every such prisoner and prisoners shall be remanded*
" *back to the prison or gaol from whence he, she, or they was or*
" *were so brought up, there to continue in execution;* but if
" any failure shall at any time be made in the payment of
" the weekly sum which shall be ordered by any such court
" to be paid to any such prisoner, such prisoner, upon ap-
" plication in term time to the court where the suit in
" which any such prisoner shall be charged in execution
" was commenced or shall have been carried on, or in the
" prison of which court any such prisoner shall stand com-
" mitted on any *habeas corpus*, or in vacation time to any
" judge of any such court, may, by the order of any such
" court or judge, be discharged out of custody on every
" such execution, proof being made before such court or
" judge on oath of the non-payment for any week of the
" sum of money ordered ' and agreed to be weekly
" paid; but every such prisoner and prisoners, before
" he, she, or they shall be so discharged out of cus-
" tody by any such rule or order, shall execute an assign-
" ment and conveyance of his, her, or their estates and
" effects in manner hereinbefore directed: and if any
" prisoner who shall petition or apply for his, her, or
" their discharge under this act, shall refuse to take the
" said

APPENDIX.

" said oath hereinbefore directed to be taken, or taking
" the same, shall afterwards be detected before any such
" court or judge of falsity therein, or shall refuse to exe-
" cute such assignment and conveyance of his, her, or their
" estates and effects as aforesaid, as hereinbefore is requir-
" ed to be made by him, her, or them respectively, he,
" she, or they shall be presently remanded and continue
" in execution.——Sect. 14. Provided always, and be
" it further enacted, That when more creditors than one
" shall charge any prisoner or prisoners in execution, *and*
" *shall desire to have such prisoner or prisoners detained in prison,*
" each and every such creditor and creditors shall only re-
" spectively pay such weekly sum of money, not exceeding
" one shilling and six pence a week, on every Monday in
" every week, to or for such respective prisoner, as the
" court before whom any such prisoner or prisoners shall
" be brought up to be discharged, shall at the time of his,
" her, or their being remanded, on such note for the pay-
" ment of the weekly sum ordered to be paid being given,
" direct or appoint."

The rest of the act is taken up with the proceedings appointed to be followed for disposing of the insolvent's effects, and distributing the produce among the creditors—purposes which cannot in any case be accomplished without the necessity of many and very complicated proceedings; and yet it can hardly be supposed that there are many imprisoned insolvents under the description of this act whose effects amount to any thing upon which those provisions can operate. But it is impossible to draw a line. Laws which aim, with minute and trivial attentions, to accomplish too much, soon end in nothing. In *many* cases it seems impossible to observe them, and therefore they come to be neglected in *all.*

NOTE

NOTE II, p. 113.

In May 1773 a fociety was inftituted for the relief and difcharge of *unfortunate* perfons imprifoned for fmall debts throughout England. Lord Romney was prefident; and Lord Vifcount Beauchamp, Lord Chief Baron Smythe, Mr. Juftice Nares, and John Thornton, Efq; were vice-prefidents. They had before received benefactions, and acted upon the plan then adopted; fo that they began, as a regular fociety, with a report of proceedings during the courfe of no more than fifteen months preceding, which cannot but appear extremely ftriking. They had, with only £.2892. 19s. 4d. difcharged no fewer than 986 prifoners, who had 566 wives and 2389 children; that is, they had in the courfe of *fifteen months* relieved from a ftate of mifery very near *four thoufand perfons*; the greater number of whom were *manufacturers, feamen,* and *labourers.*——

This is a remarkable fact, which can hardly fail to produce a very ftrong impreffion on every reflecting mind.

The fociety went on, and ftill proceed with equal fuccefs and effect. They publifh annually a ftatement of their proceedings; and the following extract from their laft year's account may be confidered not only as curious, but extremely pertinent to the prefent fubject.

The account was figned by the members prefent at their general court, held the 5th of May 1790, and the following perfons are there mentioned as forming that court:

The Right Hon. Lord Romney, *Prefident.*
The Right Hon. Earl Radnor,
The Right Hon. Lord Vifcount Beauchamp, } *Vice-Prefidents.*
The Hon. Philip Pufey,
Sir Charles Middleton, Bart.
  James Neild, Efq; *Treafurer,*
  Sir Jofeph Andrews, Bart.
  Rev. John Hunt,

APPENDIX.

Rev. John Grindley,
Gustavus Adolphus Kempenfelt, Esq;
William Townsend, Esq;
Joseph Waring, Esq;
Frederick Mathew, Esq;
Josiah Dorniford, Esq;
Mr. Thomas Dawes,
Mr. Samuel Welchman,
Mr. Charles Steuart,
Mr. Grassiwell, *Secretary*.

It exhibits the following interesting view of the proceedings from the beginning:

	N° of debtors discharged.	£.	s.	d.
From 1772 to 1774—	1722 for the sum of 4622	17	1
1775—	996	1724	1	11
1776—	673	1842	13	3
1777—	877	1729	19	7
1778—	779	1764	0	11
1779—	811	1611	15	3
1780—	628	1288	17	1
1781—	321	828	15	9
1782—	389	935	3	9
1783—	547	1121	12	0
1784—	535	996	12	3
1785—	463	904	9	1
1786—	339	715	8	9
1787—	343	749	0	10
1788—	710	1566	4	$2\frac{1}{4}$
1789—	612	1926	3	$3\frac{1}{4}$
1790—	798	2303	9	$3\frac{1}{4}$

11543
—who had 7112 wives
and 21531 children.

40186 { Persons immediately benefited, for } 26631 4 $3\frac{1}{4}$

APPENDIX.

That upwards of *forty thousand* persons should have been relieved at the expence of little more, upon the average, than *forty shillings* each debtor, and not above *thirteen shillings* (as the account states) for each individual of the families belonging to the debtors released, is a fact which warrants many inferences. But in order to give it its proper weight, some particulars, from the society's plan and minutes, must be stated.

They *compound* the debt; and the highest composition for any one debt is *ten pounds*. They give many instances of persons who had never been suspected or accused of any act of dishonesty, and had nevertheless lain *for years* in prison for a sum which they were able, according to these rules, to compound for ten pounds. One instance may be mentioned to shew the extreme folly as well as cruelty of such conduct. A young man who had an employment in one of the public offices, with a wife and five children, having been unable to discharge some demands for the support of his family, was arrested and detained in prison for several sums, amounting altogether to little more than *a hundred pounds*. He lost his employment; his situation was hopeless; his family destitute; and his petty debts were of course irrecoverably lost—yet his creditors were still keeping him in gaol, when the society interposed. He had been a prisoner for *fifteen months*, and they released him for *six pounds!*—Such cases require no commentary.

To shew that they do not proceed blindly, and without proper enquiries, it is one of their rules " that each peti-
" tioner shall be obliged to name two reputable house-
" keepers as vouchers for his integrity, sobriety, and in-
" dustry; to whom the society constantly refer their en-
" quiries, and by this means preclude almost the possibility of
" imposition."—And " any *attempt* to impose on the society
" in any particular will prevent the petitioner's being
" relieved."

Their leading rule, with regard to the objects of their charity,

charity, is in the following words: "That such debtors "shall have the preference as are most aged or infirm; "have the largest families unprovided for; are the most "likely to be useful to the community, and appear to have "lost their liberty by unavoidable misfortunes; *at least* "*not by fraud, vice, or extravagance.*"

The society extend in particular their bounty to all the *country* gaols, where, to use their own words (and they speak from experience) "a prisoner is frequently confined "at a distance of eighteen or twenty miles from his place "of abode. The creditor, for want of importunity, *forgets* "*him*; and the miserable being himself can receive no "temporary relief from his family or his friends."

To those who think lightly of the consequences ascribed to the present laws of civil imprisonment, as tending to deprive the country of many useful hands, and to load multitudes with unmerited and unavailing distress, this note is directed. Facts attested by such men as are at the head of this society, supersede the necessity of innumerable cases which might be stated to the same purpose; and afford the best possible evidence that thousands of unfortunate families are irretrievably ruined by the regular operation of laws which were intended for the purposes of justice.

NOTE KK, p. 128.

It is but a few years since the practice was thus justly and rationally settled—for it was formerly held, that a plaintiff who resided in a foreign country, or beyond the reach of the laws of England, could not be obliged to give security for eventual costs. In Michaelmas term 1774, in the case of *Nundcomar* v. *Burdett*, where the plaintiff resided at *Calcutta*, in the *East Indies*, a motion was made by Mr.
Willes,

Willes, on the part of the defendant, to stay proceedings till security should be given for eventual costs, and (in the absence of *Lord Mansfield*) the motion received this answer from Mr. Justice *Aston*: " It is every day refused—I " have many notes of its being so." *Cowper*, 158.—And there are indeed in the books many such cases. But a similar motion having been made in the case of a plaintiff residing in *Georgia*, in *North America*, and opposed upon those former cases, the court granted the rule; and Mr. Justice *Buller* expressed himself thus: " There have been
" several late cases to the contrary; and for this reason,
" that if a verdict be given against the plaintiff, he is not
" within the reach of our law, so as to have process served
" upon him for the costs." 1 *Term Reports*, 267.—And the law upon this point of practice was fully and comprehensively stated by the same learned judge, in a case of ejectment, as follows: " There are only three instances
" in which the court will interfere on behalf of a defendant
" to oblige the plaintiff to give security for costs. The
" first is, when an infant sues, the court will oblige the
" *prochein amy*, or guardian, or attorney, to give security
" for the costs: 2dly, *When the plaintiff resides abroad*, in
" which case the court will stay the proceedings till se-
" curity is given for the costs: and, 3dly, Where there
" has been a former ejectment; but there the rule is to
" stay the proceedings in the second ejectment till the
" costs of the former are paid, and till security is given for
" the costs of the second."—1 *Term Reports*, 491.

To extend the application of the principle upon which this practice proceeds, by empowering the courts, when defendants are imprisoned, to require of plaintiffs, in certain circumstances, security for eventual damages as well as costs, is one of the objects of that part of the plan to which this note refers.

www.ingramcontent.com/pod-product-compliance
Lightning Source LLC
Chambersburg PA
CBHW031811230426
43669CB00009B/1102